America the Beautiful?

The United States in Bible Prophecy

And the Lord, the God of their fathers, sent word to them again and again by His messengers, because He had compassion on His people . . . but they continually despised His words and scoffed at His prophets, until the wrath of the Lord arose against His people, until there was no remedy. — 2 Chronicles 36:15-16

Dr. David R. Reagan

LAMB & LION MINISTRIES

McKinney, Texas

Dedicated to

Jim & Darlene Bridges

in appreciation for their encouragement
and support.

First edition, 2003
Second Edition, 2006
Third Edition, 2009

Copyright © 2009 by Lamb & Lion Ministries

ISBN: 978-0-945593-17-1

Library of Congress Control Number: 2009902951

Lamb & Lion Ministries
P.O. Box 919
McKinney, Texas 75070
lamblion@lamblion.com
www.lamblion.com

Cover design by Keith Fink of Master's Press
in Dallas, Texas.

All scripture quotations are from the New American Standard
Version, © 1995 by the Lockman Foundation.

Printed in the United States of America.

America the Beautiful?

The United States in Bible Prophecy

Sam + Marilynn –
I praise ~~God~~ for the
~~you~~ call He has
placed on your lives
with Jews for Jesus.
Boruch Haba Bishem
Adonai!
Shalom in Yeshua,
Dave Reagan
7/09

Contents

Books by Dr. David R. Reagan

(Most of these have been published in languages other than English)

The Christ in Prophecy Study Guide (McKinney, TX: Lamb & Lion Ministries, 1987). Second edition in 2001.

Trusting God: Learning to Walk by Faith (Lafeyette, LA: Huntington House, 1987). Second edition in 1994.

Jesus is Coming Again! (Eugene, OR: Harvest House, 1992).

The Master Plan: Making Sense of the Controversies Surrounding Bible Prophecy Today (Eugene, OR: Harvest House, 1993).

Living for Christ in the End Times (Green Forest, AR: New Leaf Press, 2000).

Wrath and Glory: Unveiling the Majestic Book of Revelation (Green Forest, AR: New Leaf Press, 2001).

America the Beautiful? The United States in Bible Prophecy (McKinney, TX: Lamb & Lion Ministries, 2003). Second edition in 2006. Third edition in 2009.

God's Plan for the Ages: The Blueprint of Bible Prophecy (McKinney, TX: Lamb & Lion Ministries, 2005).

Preface

When I was 20 years old, God called me into the ministry. Unlike Isaiah who said, "Here am I, Lord, send me," I said, "Here am I, Lord, send anyone but me."

For the next 20 years I ran from the Lord. During that time, I pursued a career in higher education, teaching international politics at the university level. I enjoyed a lot of success, but I was never fulfilled because I was out of the Lord's will.

Finally, in 1980, while I was serving as vice president of a university, the Lord brought me to the end of myself, and I decided to step out in faith, abandon my academic career, and establish a Bible prophecy ministry. Since that time I have devoted myself to proclaiming the soon return of Jesus.

As I look back over those 20 years I spent wandering in my own personal wilderness, I can see that even when I was running from the Lord, He was preparing me for the ministry that He would ultimately entrust to me. For you see, end time Bible prophecy is all about international politics!

World Politics in the Bible

I have a better grasp of world politics now than I ever had when I was teaching it full time in the secular world. That's because I now approach it from God's perspective because I base my observations and conclusions on His Word.

I have discovered that the Hebrew prophet Daniel, who wrote 600 years before Christ, was the most astute observer of world politics who has ever lived. He advised the king of Babylon on affairs of state, and in his writings he presented an in-depth analysis of God's relationship with the nations of the world. By the inspiration of God, he wrote a history of world empires before they even existed! With absolute historical precision, he prophesied that the Babylonian Empire would be overthrown by the Medo-Persians, who would give way to the Greeks, who, in turn, would succumb to the Romans.

The Nations in Prophecy

Daniel was not the only Old Testament prophet who wrote about world politics. Almost all of them wrote about Judah and Israel and their ultimate fates. They also produced a plethora of prophecies regarding many other nations — like Syria, Ethiopia, Egypt, Saudi Arabia, Lebanon, Persia, Ammon, Edom, and Moab.

The prophets also spoke frequently about the end time world political scene that would exist right before the Messiah's return to establish his earthly reign. The foundation of all these prophecies is the re-establishment of Israel, after which that nation becomes the focal point of world politics.

The Great Omission

The end time prophecies are given in detail. They concern the Arabs, Russia, the Far East, and Western Europe. But they seem to be strangely silent about the Western Hemisphere and the United States.

How could that be? How could the prophets fail to mention the world's greatest power in the end times? Does that mean historically that we are not really in the end times? Or, does it mean the United States will suddenly cease to exist? And, if so, why and how?

These and many other questions about the destiny of the United States are the concern of this book. As we pursue the answers to these questions, I pray you will be driven into God's Word and drawn into a closer relationship with His Son, Jesus, who is our Blessed Hope.

Maranatha!

Dr. David R. Reagan
Allen, Texas
Spring of 2003

Second Edition

In the three years since this book was first published, I have received many communications thanking me for writing it. People have affirmed that the book has helped them considerably in understanding the relationship between Bible prophecy and end time world politics. They have also stated that the book helped them to better understand how God works among nations and how He is currently relating to the United States.

The original edition was published a year and a half after the horrendous 9/11 attacks on our nation. Since that time, our nation has experienced a second major calamity — Hurricane Katrina.

Because the book seems to have proved so valuable to so many people, and because the Hurricane Katrina disaster relates directly to the book's theme, I decided to keep the book in print but to re-publish it in a reworked and expanded second edition.

Dr. David R. Reagan
Allen, Texas
January of 2006

Third Edition

This is obviously a work in progress!

One problem I had to wrestle with concerning this revision was whether or not to rewrite the entire book or else simply update it with some additional chapters concerning the United States, the world political scene, and the way we as individual Christians should relate to both. After much soul-searching, I decided on the latter approach which, I admit, is rather novel.

What I've done is to apply dates to the sections of the book so that you will know when each portion was written — whether in 2003, 2006, or 2009. I felt this was the proper way to go because the book is an interpretation of Bible prophecy, and by leaving each section of the book as originally written, you could judge for yourself as to how accurate my interpretations have been.

But let me make one thing very clear — I do not claim to be a prophet. I am only a student of God's Prophetic Word. If I have any gift of prophecy, it is the God-given ability to understand how Bible prophecies apply to this day and time. I have no supernatural knowledge of the future.

As one of my Bible prophecy colleagues, Al Gist, often puts it, "I am not a prophet. I am not the son of a prophet. And, in fact, I work for a non-profit organization!"

The important thing to keep in mind is that a person does not have to have supernatural knowledge of the future in order to accurately predict what is going to happen. What you need is two things: knowledge of Bible prophecy and understanding of key biblical principles.

Thus, through knowledge of Bible prophecy, anyone could have predicted long ago — as many did — that one day the nation of Israel would be re-established. And through understanding of biblical principles regarding how God deals with nations, one could predict with confidence — as Dave Wilkerson has done — that this nation will soon be destroyed.

And that brings me back to what this book is all about. As I observe our nation's continuing rebellion against God, and as I evaluate the developments on the world political scene, I am convinced that a fourth edition of this book will never be published.

That's because we appear to have reached the point of no return as a nation — the point at which God delivers a rebellious nation from judgment to destruction.

We have set our face against God. We have ignored prophetic voices calling us to repentance. We have refused to pay attention to remedial judgments designed to sober us spiritually.

We are mocking the One who has blessed us so abundantly. We are thumbing our nose at His patience with us. We are begging for destruction, and we are about to experience it.

These are not words I enjoy writing. I love the United States of America, and so does God. Like ancient Judah, He raised up our nation to be a witness of Him. He has blessed us beyond any nation that has ever existed, with the exception of Judah.

But like the people of Judah, we Americans have turned our backs on the One who blessed us, and like Judah, we must pay the price for our unrelenting, unrepentant rebellion.

I have seen no change in course for our nation since I wrote the first edition of this book in 2003. Our flight from God has continued. The only change I have witnessed is a speeding up in the pace of our rebellion. We have continued to secularize and paganize, and in the process, our society has become increasingly anti-Christian.

This has caused my own personal sense of urgency to increase exponentially. The signs of the times are shouting to my heart, declaring that our nation is teetering on the precipice of disaster.

Those same signs declare that Jesus is at the very gates of Heaven, waiting for His Father's command to return.

This is no time for lethargy. The lukewarm Church needs to be awakened to the reality that Jesus is returning soon, that we are living on borrowed time, that Christians need to commit themselves to holiness and evangelism, and that the world must be called to repentance.

As prophesied in Revelation 3:15-16, the end time Church has gotten in bed with the world. It is condoning sin rather than condemning it. It is tiptoeing through the tulips, trying to avoid controversy lest it end up not being seeker-friendly.

In the meantime, millions of souls are headed to Hell, and our nation is destined to destruction.

My hope is that this fourth edition of this book will awaken each reader to the need for immediate, zealous action to prepare for the imminent return of Jesus.

Dr. David R. Reagan
Allen, Texas
March of 2009

America the Beautiful?

The United States in Bible Prophecy

2003

America the Beautiful

O beautiful for spacious skies,
For amber waves of grain,
For purple mountain majesties,
Above the fruited plain!

America! America!
God shed His grace on thee,
And crown thy good,
with brotherhood,
From sea to shining sea.

The song, "America the Beautiful," was written in 1893 by Katharine Lee Bates (1859-1929). Ms. Bates was a lifelong professor of English at Wellesley College in Massachusetts. She wrote a second version of the song in 1904. Her final version was written in 1913. The music was composed by Samuel A. Ward (1847-1903).

In the summer of 1893 she taught at Colorado College in Colorado, Springs. Here's how she described the occasion that prompted her writing of the song:

> One day some of the other teachers and I decided to go on a trip to 14,000 foot Pikes Peak. We hired a prairie wagon. Near the top we had to leave the wagon and go the rest of the way on mules. I was very tired. But when I saw the view, I felt great joy. All the wonder of America seemed displayed there, with the sea-like expanse.

Introduction

Fifty Years of Sinful Drift

I was born in 1938 when cars still had American names and running boards — and before they had air conditioning, automatic transmissions, radial tires, cruise control, power steering and brakes, and turning signals.

When I turned 50 in 1988, I sat down for a while and contemplated the changes that had taken place during those years. I was overwhelmed. I came away from the experience feeling like an antique.

Technological Changes

I was reminded again and again of the prophecy in Daniel 12:4 which says that in the end times men will move about quickly and knowledge will increase.

I made a long list of all the inventions that have become commonplace in my lifetime. The most significant technological developments I could think of were television, nuclear power, the computer, and space travel. (The Internet at that time was unknown to me.)

The first television set I remember seeing was in 1952. A radio station in my home town of Waco, Texas set up a circus tent full of TV sets, and people paid one dollar to watch the Republican National Convention. We mainly saw "snow" as the picture drifted in and out.

Societal Changes

Equally significant to me were the societal developments I could think of during the past 50 years. When I was born:

- Abortionists were sent to prison.
- Pregnancy out of marriage was thought of as scandalous.
- Homosexuality was considered a perversion.
- Pornography was despised as moral filth.
- Marriage was sacred. Living together was taboo. Divorce was a disgrace.
- Homemaking was honored, and day care was provided by mothers in their homes.
- Child abuse was almost unheard of.
- Ladies did not smoke or curse.
- "Damn" was considered flagrant language in a movie.
- Houses and autos were never locked.
- A man's word was his honor.
- Drugs were something you bought at a pharmacy (or "drug store").
- Alcoholism was considered a sin, not a disease.
- Popular music was devoid of demonic beats and words.
- Eastern religion was still in the East.
- Public school students prayed in their classes and read the Bible, and creation could still be taught as an alternative to evolution.
- Kids were spanked by parents and teachers for disobedience.
- High School graduates could read their diplomas.
- The Ten Commandments were still legal.
- "Gay" was an attitude.

- "Aids" (often translated "helps") was a gift of the Spirit (1 Corinthians 12:28).

- Our governments — local, state, and national — still promoted Judeo-Christian values rather than lotteries, horse racing, and casino gambling.

- Debt, whether public or private, was considered a disgrace.

- Christian teaching focused on sacrificing for Christ rather than confessing materialistic success.

- Governmental authority was respected. Police were held in high esteem.

- Humanism was considered a curse.

- Social security was a job. Living on welfare was unheard of.

- "1984" was a terrifying novel, not a reality.

As the Virginia Slim cigarette ad once put it, "We've come a long way, baby!" Yes, we have, and most of it has been in the wrong direction.

A Path to Destruction

Like the ancient nation of Judah, we have been blessed like no other nation. But also like Judah, we have taken pride in our blessings and have turned our back on the One who provided the blessings.

We have become a proud, arrogant and carnal nation wallowing in materialism and indulging in the pursuit of pleasure. In the process we have become the prime moral polluter of planet Earth.

Everywhere I go in the world I find the influence of our wanton immorality. All you have to do is flip on a TV set, and whether you are in Africa, Latin America, Asia or Europe, you will see the most violent and immoral American movies and television programs.

Like Judah of old, the wrath of God is hanging over our nation. God is calling us to repentance through natural signs like the eruption of Mount St. Helens in 1980, the severe drought of 1987, Hurricane Andrew in 1992, the record floods of 1993, and the unprecedented forest fires of 2002. He is also speaking to us through prophetic voices like David Wilkerson and Donald Wildmon.

But like the citizens of Judah, we have become spiritually numb. We ignore the signs and condemn the prophetic voices. We listen instead to pillow prophets who speak peace and urge us to seek the good life of health, wealth and power. We even pat ourselves on the back by reminding our critics that we are a "Christian nation."

A Christian Nation?

What a blasphemy it is to call ourselves a Christian nation! We are anything but Christ-like as we export our gross immorality to the rest of the world and murder our babies here at home at the incredible rate of more than a million and a half a year.

Our nation is a stench in the nostrils of God! If we do not repent, the wrath of God is going to be poured out upon us, and it will be severe, for those to whom much is given, much is expected. The challenge of the hour is for all of us who profess Christ to get on our knees and seek God in prayer, repenting of our wicked ways so that He will heal our land (2 Chronicles 7:14).

A Nation with Hope?

What is going to be the fate of our nation? Glory or disgrace? Will it be "America the beautiful" or America the hideous?

Does the Bible provide any clues as to what our country's fate will be? Does it contain specific prophecies about

America and its destiny?

I have been conducting prophetic conferences for the past 30 years all over the United States and around the world. That experience has impressed upon me the fact that the fate of America is the number one question of Bible prophecy. Over and over I have been asked by both American and foreign audiences, "Where is the United States in Bible prophecy?"

The Question Accentuated

The question has become even more pressing and intriguing since the collapse of the Soviet Union in 1991. Now that America is clearly the world's dominant super power, people are wondering even more than before why the Bible seems to be silent regarding the United States in the end times.

How could the biblical prophets overlook the role of the world's most powerful nation in the end times? Does America's dominance and its lack of correspondence with end time Bible prophecy mean that we really aren't living in the end times? On the other hand, could it be that America is poised for sudden destruction, and the Bible's silence is due to the fact that our nation will not be a major player on the world scene when all the end time events take place? Or, is America really in the prophetic scriptures, but in some mysterious, symbolic sense?

Let's go to God's Word and begin a search to see if we can find the United States in prophecy.

God Bless America

God Bless America,
Land that I love.
Stand beside her, and guide her
Thru the night with a light from above.
From the mountains, to the prairies,
To the oceans, white with foam,
God bless America,
My home sweet home.

"God Bless America" is the unofficial national anthem of the United States. Unlike the official national anthem, it is singable by the average person, and people love to sing it.

The song was composed by Irving Berlin (1888-1989) who immigrated with his parents from Siberia when he was only five years old.

The song was written in the summer of 1918 at Camp Upton, located in Yaphank, New York on Long Island. It was intended for a Ziegfeld-style revue, but Berlin decided that its solemn tone was out of step with the comedic nature of the show, so he laid it aside.

Twenty years later in the fall of 1938, Berlin remembered the song, made some alterations in the words, and released it. Kate Smith introduced this revised version on a radio broadcast on Armistice Day, 1938, and the song became an immediate sensation.

Chapter 1

God and the Nations:
Who is in control?

"The Lord is the true God;
He is the living God and the everlasting King.
At His wrath the earth quakes,
And the nations cannot endure His indignation."
Jeremiah 10:10

The most popular American author of the 19th Century was Mark Twain. Yet, despite all his success, there was one item he wrote that he was afraid to publish.

It was a poem entitled, "The War Prayer." He read it to his daughter, Jean, and she counseled him against publishing it because she said it would be considered sacrilegious.

Twain agreed. "I have told the whole truth in that poem," he said, "and only dead men can tell the truth in this world." And so he requested that the poem not be published until after his death. He died in 1910. The poem was not published until 1923. Its release was undoubtedly delayed by the outbreak of World War I.

A "Sacrilegious" Poem

Twain's fears were well grounded, for the poem attacked one of the most powerful false religions that Satan has ever produced — namely, the religion of nationalism.

The poem begins by describing its setting as "a time of great and exalting excitement:"

> The country was up in arms,
> The war was on,
> In every breast
> Burned the holy fire of patriotism;
> The drums were beating,
> The bands playing,
> The toy pistols popping,
> The bunched firecrackers
> Hissing and spluttering . . .

In churches across the land, "pastors preached devotion to flag and country and invoked the God of Battles," beseeching His aid in the nation's good cause. People sang to "God the all-terrible," pleading with Him to ordain their nation to victory.

A Long Prayer

And then, in the church featured in the poem, the pastor leads a "long prayer." Here is how Twain describes it:

> None could remember the like of it
> For passionate pleading
> And moving and beautiful language.
> The burden of its supplication was
> That an ever-merciful and benignant
> Father of us all would watch over
> Our noble young soldiers
> And aid, comfort, and encourage them
> In their patriotic work . . .

> Make them strong and confident,
> Invincible in the bloody onset;
> Help them to crush the foe,
> Grant to them
> And to their flag and country
> Imperishable honor and glory.

A Mysterious Stranger

At that point an aged stranger enters the church dressed like an Old Testament prophet. He quietly ascends the podium, moves to the preacher's side, and waits for him to complete his prayer with the words, "Bless our armies, grant us the victory, O Lord our God, Father and Protector of our land and flag! Amen."

As the preacher opens his eyes, he is startled by the stranger standing beside him. Before he can say another word, the stranger motions for him to sit, and then the stranger bellows, "I come from the Throne — bringing a message from Almighty God!" He proceeds to explain that he has been commissioned by God to explain what the pastor has just prayed for. The true meaning of the prayer is then translated as follows:

O Lord our God,
Help us
To tear their soldiers
To bloody shreds
With our shells;

Help us
To cover their smiling fields
With the pale forms
Of their patriot dead;

Help us
To drown the thunder
Of the guns
With the shrieks
Of their wounded
Writhing in pain;

Help us
To lay waste
Their humble homes
With a hurricane of fire;

> Help us
> To wring the hearts
> Of their unoffending widows
> With unavailing grief;

> Help us
> To turn them out roofless
> With their little children
> To wander unfriended
> The wastes
> Of their desolated land
> In rags and hunger and thirst . . .

Then, as the congregation sits dumbfounded, the stranger concludes his translation of the pastor's prayer with these words:

> For our sakes who adore Thee, Lord,
> Blast their hopes,
> Blight their lives,
> Protract their bitter pilgrimage,
> Make heavy their steps,
> Water their way with their tears . . .

> We ask it in the spirit of love,
> Of Him Who is the Source of Love . . .
> Amen.

Concluding by declaring once again that he has given them the true meaning of the pastor's prayer, the stranger asks if they still desire it. Twain concludes the poem with this statement: "It was believed afterward that the man was a lunatic, because there was no sense in what he said."

The Religion of Nationalism

Throughout history people have worshiped empires and nation-states. Repeatedly, people have given their ultimate loyalty to these collective entities which have embodied their language, culture, and values.

This loyalty has produced a religious spirit of nationalism that has been manifested in a blind and zealous patriotism that can best be summed up in the slogan, "My country, right or wrong!"

Hundreds of millions of lives have been slaughtered on the battlefields of the world, often for no other purpose than to advance the glory of their empire or nation. The religion of nationalism demands absolute loyalty, including a willingness to sacrifice one's life for the sake of the nation, regardless of the cause or purpose.

The Rise and Fall of Nations

What does the Bible have to say about the empires and nations which all of us tend to glorify and adore? The fact of the matter is that the Bible has a lot to say.

The first spiritual principle the Bible reveals is that God Himself is the one who raises up and defines the nations. To put it another way, God is the one who establishes each nation and determines its boundaries.

Paul spoke of this truth in his sermon at Athens. He asserted that God was the one who created the nations, established "the boundaries of the habitation," and "determined their appointed times" (Acts 17:26). This statement is based on a verse in Deuteronomy 32 which states that "when the Most High gave the nations their inheritance, when He separated the sons of man, He set the boundaries of the peoples . . ." (Deuteronomy 32:8).

Every nation that exists was established by God, its boundaries are God-ordained, and its time of existence has been appointed by God. Nations do not have a life of their own.

The Fall of the Mighty

The second spiritual principle revealed in the Scriptures regarding the nations is a corollary of the first. Just as God is the one who raises up each nation, He is the one who decides when a nation will cease to exist. This principle is clearly established in one of the oldest books in the Bible: "He [God] makes the nations great, then destroys them. He enlarges the nations, then leads them away" (Job 12:23).

The power of a nation is thus irrelevant if God decides that the time has come for the nation to cease to exist. The ancient empire of Babylon is a good example of this principle. At the height of its power, while the leaders were celebrating its glory, God allowed the Meades and Persians to conquer the city without a siege. They simply dammed up the river running through the city and then got down into the riverbed and marched underneath the walls!

Another good example of how God can defeat the most powerful of nations is found in 2 Kings 18 and 19. Sennacherib, the King of Assyria, sent a mammoth army to conquer the city of Jerusalem. The King of Judah, Hezekiah, knew the city could not defend itself, so he turned to the Lord in prayer and cried out for deliverance. That night, "the angel of the Lord" struck the camp of the Assyrians (probably with a plague), and 185,000 died before morning. Sennacherib fled back to Ninevah where he was assassinated while worshiping his false god, Nisroch.

One of the most unusual battle plans God ever used to put down nations is revealed in 2 Chronicles 20. The nation of Judah, under King Jehoshaphat, was being attacked by a coalition of Moabites and Ammonites. A prophet by the name of Jahaziel assured Jehoshaphat that God would defeat the enemy nations. "Do not fear or be dismayed," he said, "because of this great multitude, for the battle is not yours but God's" (2 Chronicles 20:15).

Incredibly, Jehoshaphat was instructed to hold back his army and send forth, instead, a team of praise worshipers to confront the invading armies! Jehoshaphat did as instructed, and as the praise team went forth dancing, shouting, and singing, the enemy soldiers became so confused that they panicked and turned on each other, destroying one another.

Succumbing to God's Sovereignty

Apart from the Bible, history is full of examples of mighty nations that have been humiliated, defeated, or destroyed by lesser powers. Consider Colonial America against mighty England. Or the United States against Vietnam.

Sometimes God brings down great empires from within, due to moral corruption. This is what happened to the Roman Empire. And, of course, we have a contemporary example that should be very sobering. In 1991 the Soviet Union, which at that time was the world's greatest military power with over 30,000 nuclear warheads, collapsed overnight due to moral rot and corruption within.

When God decrees the humiliation, defeat, or destruction of a nation, God's purpose will be accomplished, regardless of the nation's power. David fully recognized the truth of God's sovereignty over the nations, and he wrote about it frequently in his psalms. In Psalm 20:7 he observed, "Some boast in chariots, and some in horses; but we will boast in the name of the Lord our God." In other words, military power is useless when it is opposed to God's will. Continuing with the same theme, David wrote these words in Psalm 33:16-17 —

> 16 The king is not saved by a mighty army;
> A warrior is not delivered by great strength.

> 17 A horse is a false hope for victory;
> Nor does it deliver anyone by its great strength.

That passage reminds me of the final scene in Shakespeare's play, *Richard III*, when the king is about to die on the battlefield. In total desperation, he cries out, "A horse! A horse! My kingdom for a horse."

Why Nations Exist

A third spiritual principle regarding nations is that God has a purpose for each nation. There is an overall purpose for each nation as well as specific purposes which God may call a nation to fulfill from time to time. All of which is reminiscent of how God has given all churches the responsibility to preach the Gospel, but He calls each individual church to specialized ministries like feeding the homeless or providing a Christian school.

The overall purpose of all nations was revealed by Paul in his sermon at Athens. The nations exist for the purpose of enabling their people to seek God (Acts 17:27). They are to do this by providing an atmosphere of tranquility so that godliness might abound (1 Timothy 2:2). They exist for the purpose of punishing evildoers and rewarding those who do right (1 Peter 2:13-14).

But from time to time, God will call nations to perform specific purposes. The greatest example is, of course, Israel. God called Israel to be a witness of Him (Isaiah 43:10,12 and 44:8). They were to witness the glory of God among the nations by illustrating that when a nation is obedient to God, that nation is greatly blessed. This is one of the reasons that Israel is referred to as being "the center of the nations" (Ezekiel 5:5 and 38:12).

Now, in regard to Israel, God used some nations to bless them, while He called others to test them, discipline them, or judge them. During the time of the United Kingdom under King Solomon, the nation of Lebanon was a blessing to Israel. Hiram, the King of Tyre, sent lumber and skilled craftsmen to assist the Jews in the building of the Temple (2 Chronicles 2:11-13). In contrast, God often worked through the Philistines to test the Jews (1 Samuel 13:5-7 and 1 Chronicles

14:8-17). He sent the Egyptians to discipline them (2 Chronicles 12:9). And after the Jews split into two nations, Judah and Israel, God raised up Assyria and Babylon to judge them by destroying their nations and taking them into captivity (1 Chronicles 5:25-26 and 2 Chronicles 36:15-20).

In regard to specialized purposes, have you ever pondered what unique role God might have had in mind for the United States when He raised it up as a nation? Looking back on the first 200 years of our history, I have concluded that God's special purpose for America was to evangelize the world for Jesus. He has worked through our incredible natural resources and technical ingenuity to translate the Bible into many languages and to proclaim the Gospel to the world through radio, television, movies, video programs, and audio tapes.

Let's pause for a review:

● God establishes the nations and defines their boundaries.

● God determines when a nation will cease to exist.

● God has a purpose for each nation — both general and specific.

Blessings and Curses

The fourth spiritual principle regarding nations is revealed in Deuteronomy 28. In that passage, speaking through Moses, God makes it clear that He blesses and disciplines nations in accordance with their obedience to Him.

This principle applies in particular to the way in which nations treat the Jewish people. God made this clear in the Abrahamic Covenant when He promised that He would bless those who bless the Jews and curse those who curse them (Genesis 12:3). In fulfillment of this promise, history is littered with the carcasses of states which have persecuted the Jewish people — like Nazi Germany and Soviet Russia.

A classic historical example of this principle in operation can be found in the history of Spain. That nation reached its zenith of world power in the 15th Century under the leadership of Ferdinand and Isabella. But in 1492, the same year they dispatched Columbus on his historic voyage, they ruthlessly expelled all the Jews from Spain. That act proved to be the beginning of the end of the Spanish empire.

When a nation walks in God's ways, He prospers it with great leaders who provide freedom and prosperity. When a nation rebels against God's commandments, He places curses, or remedial judgments, upon the people. Deuteronomy 28 spells out a wide variety of these judgments, including such things as confusing government policies, economic weakness, rebellious youth, rampant disease, crop failures, an epidemic of divorce, foreign domination, and defeat in war.

Determining National Leadership

In accordance with this principle, I believe God gives a nation the kind of leaders it deserves. Consider for example the histories of Israel and Judah. When the United Kingdom of David and Solomon broke up, the northern nation of Israel (consisting of ten tribes) was born in rebellion and idolatry, and it continued to wallow in idolatry throughout its history. Accordingly, during its 208 years of existence, the nation did not have one king who was considered righteous in the eyes of God. Because the people were determined to live in rebellion and serve idols, God provided them with leaders who were cruel and selfish (2 Kings 17:7-18).

In contrast, the people living in the southern nation of Judah (consisting of two tribes plus the Levites) had a heart for God and His Word. They sought to please the Lord, and He responded by giving them eight righteous kings out of a total of 20. He also extended the life of their nation, giving them an additional 136 years beyond the fall of Israel to the Assyrians. But the nation ultimately became a victim of pride.

The people began to view their blessings as their own accomplishment. Their zeal for God grew cold. Their religion became an exercise in hypocrisy.

The Example of Manasseh

To get their attention, God raised up one of the most immoral and corrupt leaders in biblical history — King Manasseh. He was a gross idolater, a blasphemer, and a person who dabbled in astrology and witchcraft. He also committed the horrible evil of sacrificing his children to demons by burning them alive (2 Chronicles 33:1-7).

The oppressive rule of this evil man must have driven many of the people of Judah to their knees in repentance, crying out to God for deliverance. I say that because Manasseh was followed by a godly king. God had specified years before in a statement to King Solomon that the only way to heal a sinful nation is through prayer on the part of godly people: "[If] My people who are called by My name humble themselves and pray and seek My face and turn from their wicked ways, then I will hear from heaven, will forgive their sin and will heal their land" (2 Chronicles 7:14).

The godly king the Lord provided after Manasseh was Josiah who ascended the throne at the tender age of eight. The Word says that when he was 16 "he began to seek the God of his father David," and when he was 20 he began to purge the land of idols (2 Chronicles 34:1-3). The result was the greatest spiritual revival recorded in the Old Testament histories.

Unfortunately, however, sin had become so ingrained in the culture, that when Josiah was killed in a battle 19 years later, the nation quickly reverted back to its rebellion against God's Word. The Lord responded by supplying a quick succession of four evil kings before He delivered the nation from judgment to destruction at the hands of the Babylonians.

The Principle Applied to America

A look at the recent history of the United States reveals that God still deals with nations in the same manner. This nation began its intense rebellion against God during the free love decade of the 1960's. As we began to shake our collective fist at God and mock His commandments, look at the series of leaders He provided us with:

- John F. Kennedy — the hedonistic philanderer
- Lyndon Johnson — the unbridled egotist
- Richard Nixon — the sordid schemer
- Gerald Ford — the inept bumbler
- Jimmy Carter — the deceived humanist

As Christians began to cry out for deliverance, repenting of the sins of their nation, God finally responded by blessing the nation with a great leader, Ronald Reagan. He restored dignity to the office, gave the nation renewed vision, won the Cold War, and laid the foundation for the greatest stretch of economic prosperity the nation has ever experienced.

But his successor, George Bush, became deceived by the vision of a "New World Order," and in the process, he turned against the nation of Israel, forcing the Jewish leaders to begin the suicidal appeasement policy of trading land for peace.

Bush's policies were spiritual disasters. His constant prattling about a "New World Order" served to pave the way for American acceptance of One World policies that are destined to pave the way for the establishment of the empire of the Antichrist. And his betrayal of Israel begged for God's wrath to fall on America.

So, God limited Bush to one term and replaced him with a modern day Manasseh — Bill Clinton. Clinton came into office promoting homosexuality and abortion. He ceased the prosecution of pornographers. He encouraged the filth of

Hollywood. He demeaned the office of the President with his clownish and vulgar lifestyle. He undermined American sovereignty with a spate of treaties designed to promote the philosophy of One Worldism. And he continued to strong-arm Israel to surrender its God-given territory.

Once again, Christians were driven to their knees, repenting of America's immorality, violence, and blasphemy, while calling on God for dignified, moral leadership. And once again, God in His mercy heard and responded by miraculously orchestrating the election of a born again Christian, George W. Bush.

The Bible clearly teaches that God is the one who raises up the leaders of the nations, and He is the one who brings them down (Daniel 2:21 and Romans 13:1). And often, He gives us the kind of leaders we deserve.

God's Attitude Toward the Nations

The fifth spiritual principle that must be understood regarding the nations of the world is that God holds them in contempt. This principle seems on the surface to be contradictory in nature. After all, God is the one who creates the nations and uses them for His purposes. Why, then, does He hold them in contempt?

Let's first of all establish the fact that God really does hold the nations in contempt. Consider this passage in Isaiah 40:15,17 —

> 15 Behold, the nations are like a drop from a bucket . . .

> 17 All the nations are as nothing before Him,
> They are regarded by Him as less than nothing
> and meaningless.

These are jolting words because they stand in stark contrast to the attitude of Mankind. People all over the world adore and worship their nations. But God holds them in contempt.

This fact was emphasized to the prophet Daniel in two very contrasting visions — one given to King Nebuchadnezzer and the other to Daniel himself.

In Nebuchadnezzer's dream he saw a statue that "was large and of extraordinary splendor . . . and its appearance was awesome" (Daniel 2:31). The head was made of gold, the chest was silver, the thighs were bronze, and the legs were iron. Daniel interpreted the dream to represent a succession of world empires. He explained that the head of gold represented Nebuchadnezzer's Babylonian empire. It would be overthrown by the Medo-Persian empire which, in turn, would be destroyed by an empire based in Greece. The legs of iron represented the Roman empire that would succeed the Grecian empire of Alexander the Great (Daniel 2:31-40).

Fifty years later, Daniel was given a vision in which God presented the same succession of Gentile empires (Daniel 7:1-7). But Daniel saw them from God's perspective. Instead of a glorious image like Nebuchadnezzer saw, Daniel witnessed a series of ravenous beasts which devoured each other. First came a lion (Babylon), then a bear (Medo-Persia), and next a leopard (Greece). The fourth beast (Rome) was "dreadful and terrifying and extremely strong; and it had large iron teeth. It devoured and crushed and trampled down . . ." (Daniel 7:7).

What a contrast in viewpoints! To Man, the empires are glorious. To God, they are savage beasts.

The Basis of God's Attitude

How can God's viewpoint be explained? Well, the explanation is really very simple: the empires and nations of this world are part of Satan's kingdom.

You see, when God created the earth, He intended for Man to have dominion over everything — the plant and animal kingdoms and the nations (Genesis 1:26). But Man rebelled against God, and when he did, Satan stole the dominion intended for Man. Satan became the prince of this earth, with the nations under his dominion.

That's why Jesus referred to Satan as "the ruler of this world" (John 12:31). And that's why Satan could legitimately tempt Jesus by offering Him all the kingdoms of the world in exchange for His worship (Matthew 4:8-9). Dominion over the nations was Satan's to give.

The Struggle for Dominion

Jesus won back that dominion on the Cross, but He has not yet returned to claim it and exercise it. The writer of Hebrews says that because of the Cross, all things have been put in subjection to Jesus (Hebrews 2:8), but he quickly adds that "we do not yet see all things subjected to Him" (Hebrews 2:8) because that will not become a reality until Jesus returns. At that time, the enemies of God will be made "a footstool for His feet" (Hebrews 10:13).

So, even after the Cross, Paul called Satan "the god of this world" (2 Corinthians 4:4). Likewise, John stated "the whole world lies in the power of the evil one" (1 John 5:19).

God raises up the nations, and He is the one who puts them down. But in between their birth and death, Satan comes against them, determined to corrupt and compromise their governments so that he can control them.

The Example of Saul

This principle is illustrated in the life of King Saul. He began his rule of Israel with great promise. He was a man of physical stature who commanded respect by his very presence (1 Samuel 9:1-2). He was given a special anointing of the Holy Spirit to empower him to serve his people wisely (1 Samuel 10:6, 9-10). But Satan attacked him immediately with a spirit of melancholy that threw him into fits of depression and generated jealousy in his heart toward David.

Instead of turning to God for deliverance, Saul resorted to trafficking in demons by consulting witches. In response, the

Lord lifted His Spirit (1 Samuel 16:14), and Saul ended up by committing suicide on the battlefield. It is a tragic story that has been retold many times in the lives of political leaders throughout history.

All of which points to the reason why we are so earnestly exhorted in Scripture to pray for those in positions of authority (1 Timothy 2:1-2). When God puts a person in a governing role, Satan immediately moves that person up on his hit list and starts trying to compromise him or her so that he can control the person.

Courting God's Contempt

The result is a never-ending stream of political corruption which shapes the nature of nations, causing them to be held in contempt by God for three reasons.

The first problem is the prideful attitude that characterizes the nations of the world. Nations inevitably take pride in themselves and devote much time to self-exaltation. This is only natural since nations are composed of prideful people and are governed by prideful leaders. Nationhood always becomes an expression of collective pride, and it is condemned throughout the Bible, as in Obadiah 3 and 4 where the prophet criticizes the pride of Edom:

> 3 "The arrogance of your heart has deceived you
>   You who live in the clefts of the rock [speaking
>   of the rock city of Petra]
>   In the loftiness of your dwelling place,
>   Who say in your heart,
>   'Who will bring me down to earth?'

> 4 "Though you build high like the eagle,
>   Though you set your nest among the stars,
>   From there I will bring you down,"
>   declares the Lord.

How many leaders of nations have you ever seen take the podium at the United Nations and apologize for their national behavior? Can you imagine the Chinese apologizing to the world for the slaughter at Tiananmen Square? Or someone like Saddam Hussein asking forgiveness for his country's invasion of Kuwait? There is no pride stronger than national pride.

A Spirit of Rebellion

Another reason God holds the nations in contempt is because their pride compels them to be rebellious. Psalm 2 pictures all the nations of the world in rebellion against God and His Anointed One, the Messiah. The political leaders of the world are pictured shaking their fists at God and asking, "Who do You think You are to tell us what we can and cannot do?"

A good example of the rebellious nature of the world's nations can be found in what is called the "10/40 Window." These are the nations of the world that are located throughout Africa and Asia from 10 degrees to 40 degrees north of the equator. I have a list of these nations that I use as a daily prayer guide. There are a total of 65 nations on the list, and only 6 allow Christian evangelism. That means that in 91% of these nations it is against the law to proclaim the Gospel! Such a prohibition flies directly in the face of what Paul said is the fundamental purpose of a nation — namely, to provide an atmosphere of peace and freedom that will enable people to seek God (Acts 17:27).

The Ultimate Idol

The third reason God is contemptuous of the nations is because they stand as idols between Him and Mankind. In fact, the nation-state is Man's ultimate idol. The only thing that comes close is the willingness of people to fight and die for a religion like Islam.

To what other idol in all of history has the blood of so many millions been sacrificed? Throughout history people have been willing to die for their nation when they were unwilling to sacrifice their lives for anything else. It is no wonder that Mark Twain feared publishing his poem, "The War Prayer," for it strikes at the heart of this idolatry.

Reflecting

Let's pause again for another review:

- God establishes the nations and defines their boundaries.

- God determines when a nation will cease to exist.

- God has a purpose for each nation — both general and specific.

- God blesses and disciplines nations in accordance with their obedience to Him and their treatment of the Jewish people.

- God holds the nations in contempt because of their pride and rebellion, and because they serve as idols.

The sixth spiritual principle is that God forgives and blesses a nation when its people repent. I have already alluded to this principle, but I want to emphasize it.

Moving God's Heart

There is nothing that moves the heart of God like repentance. Biblical examples abound. I have already mentioned Judah under King Josiah (2 Chronicles 34-35). God was even willing to forgive the evil Assyrian empire when its king and the people of its capital city of Nineveh responded in repentance to the preaching of Jonah (Jonah 3).

Abe Lincoln understood this important principle. In 1863, during the Civil War, he issued an amazing presidential proclamation in which he called for "a day of national humiliation, fasting and prayer." He specifically called Americans to repentance because he said he was convinced that the war was a chastisement of God for "the presumptuous sins" of the nation. Lincoln wrote:

> We have been the recipients of the choicest boun-ties of Heaven. We have been preserved these many years in peace and prosperity. We have grown in numbers, wealth, and power as no other nation has ever grown. But we have forgotten God . . . and we have vainly imagined, in the deceitful-ness of our hearts, that all these blessings were produced by some superior wisdom and virtue of our own. Intoxicated with unbroken success, we have become too self-sufficient to feel the neces-sity of redeeming and preserving grace, too proud to pray to the God that made us.

Lincoln concluded the proclamation by setting aside Thursday, April 30, 1863, as a day for his fellow citizens to go to their places of worship "to humble ourselves before the offended Power, to confess our national sins, and to pray for clemency and forgiveness." It was one of those rare occasions in history when a national leader asked a nation to swallow its pride and humble itself before God in repentance.

The United States has become so secularized in recent years that it is almost unthinkable that an American president would issue such a proclamation today. He would be de-nounced for violating "the separation of church and state," and he would probably be subjected to impeachment proceedings.

Daniel's Example

As I have mentioned before, God in His mercy does not require that everyone in a nation repent. In 2 Chronicles 7:14 He makes it clear that He will heal any land where those who are called by His name — Christians — will humble them-selves, pray, and seek His face while turning from their wicked ways.

The prophet Daniel provided us with the kind of prayer that will move God's heart to national forgiveness and healing. It is recorded in Daniel 9.

When Daniel discovered Jeremiah's prophecy that the captivity of Israel would last 70 years (Jeremiah 25:11), he realized that time period was almost up, and he also realized that the Jews had not repented. So, he got on his knees and repented in behalf of his nation. The amazing thing about his remarkable prayer (Daniel 9:4-19) is that this righteous man took the sins of the nation upon himself. He prayed, "*we* have sinned," "*we* have rebelled," "indeed, *all* Israel has trans-gressed" (Daniel 9:5,9,11). Daniel recognized that when a nation sins, all the citizens are part of the problem, either directly (by participating in the sins) or indirectly (by failing to denounce the sins).

As I pointed out earlier, Israel is a continuing witness of what it means to have a relationship with God. Since their rebellious rejection of Jesus as their Messiah, the Jews have been under the discipline of God. But the Bible prophesies that one day a great remnant of the Jews will repent and accept Jesus as their Messiah (Zechariah 12:10), and when they do so, God will forgive and forget their rebellion and save them (Zechariah 13:1). He will then pour out His blessings upon them (Isaiah 62:1-3).

Compelling God's Wrath

The final spiritual principle concerning nations that I want to mention is that God destroys a nation when its rebellion reaches a point of no return. The trigger point that motivates God to deliver a nation from judgment to destruction is revealed in the book of Nahum.

The prophet Nahum came on the scene 150 years after Jonah. Like Jonah, he was called of God to preach to Nineveh. But, unlike Jonah, he was not sent to call the people to repentance. Rather, he was told to inform them that the time had arrived for their destruction. This warning was in accordance with God's character, for He never pours out His wrath without warning.

In Nahum 1:11 God reveals the reason for His unalterable decision to destroy the city and its empire: "From you has gone forth one who plotted evil against the Lord, a wicked counselor." Thus, the trigger point of God's wrath is when neglect or rejection of Him turns to war against Him. In response, God declared, "Your wound is incurable" (Nahum 3:19). In short, their fate was sealed.

A contemporary of Nahum's, the prophet Jeremiah, spoke of the same principle regarding God's relationship to Judah. He proclaimed that the nation's wound was "incurable" (Jeremiah 30:12). He added, "There is no one to plead your cause, no healing for your sore, no recovery for you" (Jeremiah 30:13).

The Point of No Return

One chilling point is that the Bible teaches that when a nation reaches this point of no return — this point where "the wound becomes incurable" — prayer is no longer of any avail. Thus, Jeremiah was told by God that he was not to pray for the deliverance of Judah! "Do not pray for this people, and do not lift up a cry or prayer for them, and do not intercede with Me; for I do not hear you" (Jeremiah 7:16). Later, God made this same point again in even stronger terms: "Even though Moses and Samuel were to stand before Me, My heart would not be with this people; send them away from My presence and let them go!" (Jeremiah 15:1).

Ezekiel was told the same thing when he tried to pray for Judah, but in even stronger terms. God named three of the most righteous men who had ever lived — Job, Noah, and Daniel — and He told Ezekiel that even their prayers could not deliver the nation from His wrath (Ezekiel 14:12-21). "I have set My face against them," the Lord concluded (Ezekiel

15:7).

God is patient and longsuffering. But He cannot be mocked. "Whatever you devise against the Lord, He will make a complete end of it" (Nahum 1:9). God will ultimately deal with the sin of every nation. "The Lord is slow to anger and great in power, and the Lord will by no means leave the guilty unpunished" (Nahum 1:3). Some nations will be destroyed before the Great Tribulation begins, but all nations will taste God's wrath during that terrible period of international judgment.

An Overview

Let's conclude with a final review:

* God establishes the nations and defines their bound-aries.

* God determines when a nation will cease to exist.

* God has a purpose for each nation — both general and specific.

* God blesses and disciplines nations in accordance with their obedience to Him and their treatment of the Jewish people.

* God holds the nations in contempt because of their pride and rebellion, and because they serve as idols.

* God forgives and blesses a nation when its people repent.

* God destroys a nation when its rebellion becomes entrenched, reaching a point of no return.

Looking Toward a Day of Justice

A day of reckoning for all the nations is coming. That's why God sits in the heavens and laughs over the rebellion of the world's leaders (Psalm 2:4). His laughter is not prompted by a lack of concern. No, His laughter is due to the fact that

He has appointed a day when He will "speak to them in His anger and terrify them in His fury" (Psalm 2:5). It is the day when His Son will return to reign from Mt. Zion in Jerusalem (Psalm 2:6). The nations will tremble at His presence (Isaiah 64:2), and the kings and presidents and prime ministers will hide in caves and cry out for the mountains to fall upon them (Revelation 6:15-16).

Only one nation, Israel, will retain its current identity into the millennial reign of Jesus. All others will be destroyed during the Tribulation (Jeremiah 30:11).

But we are getting ahead of ourselves. What does the Bible have to say about the nations in the end times, in the period immediately preceding the Tribulation? Is there a specific world political pattern that is spelled out which we will be able to identify? If so, where does the United States fit into the pattern? Will we continue to dominate the world scene? Or, are our days numbered as a world power?

The Star Spangled Banner
(fourth verse)

O thus be it ever when free men shall stand
Between their loved home and the war's desolation;
Blest with vict'ry and peace, may the heaven-res-
cued land
Praise the Power that hath made and preserved us a
nation!
Then conquer we must, when our cause it is just,
And this be our motto: "In God is our trust!"
And the star-spangled banner in triumph shall wave
O'er the land of the free and the home of the brave.

On September 24, 1814, a lawyer named Francis Scott Key (1780-1843) peered through clearing smoke to see an enormous flag flying proudly after a 25 hour British bombardment of Baltimore's Fort McHenry. Key was inspired to write a poem which he entitled, "Defense of Fort McHenry." The poem soon gained wide spread popularity as it was sung to the tune of a British melody called "To Anacreon in Heaven."

The song gained steadily in popularity in the years before the Civil War. By 1861 it shared with "Yankee Doodle" and "Hail Columbia" the distinction of being played on most patriotic occasions.

The song did not become the official national anthem of the United States until 1931, seven years before the more popular "God Bless America" was published.

Chapter 2

The Nations in Prophecy:
Where are they heading?

"He makes the nations great, then destroys them;
He enlarges the nations, then leads them away"
Job 12:23

Shortly after the fall of the Soviet Union in 1991, I started receiving messages from detractors who disagreed with my teachings concerning Bible prophecy. One telephone conversation went like this —

"I'm calling to ask you if you are ready to admit that you are wrong."

"Wrong about what?" I asked.

"About Russia invading Israel."

"Why should I change my conviction about that?"

"Because the Soviet Union has collapsed, and Communism is dead."

"But that doesn't change what the Bible says is going to happen in the end times."

I went on to explain that anti-Semitism is deeply rooted in Russian culture. I pointed out that the Czars were vehemently anti-Semitic long before the Communist revolution of 1917. I also emphasized that Russia has no cultural values or historical traditions to support a democratic form of government.

"Democracy has no hope in Russia," I asserted. "Sooner or later the democratic facade will give way to the rise of a dictator, and he will blame all the problems of Russia on the Jews — just as did the Czars and the Commissars."

Prophecy and World Events

The interpretation of Bible prophecy cannot be dictated by world events. If the Bible says an event is going to occur in the future — like a Russian invasion of Israel — it is going to happen, regardless of trends in world politics. The Russian invasion of Israel predicted in Bible prophecy has never been dependent upon Russia being a Communist state.

When interpreting what the Bible says about world politics in the end times, we need to have the faith that was demonstrated by C. I. Scofield when he published his famous Study Bible in 1909. He interpreted Ezekiel 38 and 39 to mean that Russia would invade Israel in the end times. That interpretation was challenged and even mocked.

Scholars asked, "How can you possibly say that these chapters prophesy a Russian invasion of Israel? Russia is a Christian Orthodox nation, and Israel doesn't even exist! Nor is there any possibility that Israel will ever exist again."

Scofield's response was simple: "I don't understand it, and I can't explain it, but the Bible says it, and therefore I believe it."

Today, one hundred years later, Israel exists and Russia is anything but a Christian nation. The Russians are currently sporting a thin democratic veneer, but underneath is an ugly heritage of dictatorship, repression, and anti-Semitism. Furthermore, the society is wallowing in economic chaos and violence as former Communist officials now operate as Mafia thugs building regional empires that are immune to government control. Another thing to keep in mind is that the central Russian republics contain an enormous Islamic population that is vehemently opposed to the state of Israel.

A Perplexing Issue

The collapse of the Soviet Union also prompted the scoffers to make another assertion: "You say we are on the threshold of the Tribulation, but with the fall of Soviet Russia, the United States now stands as the world's only super power. Since America is dominating the world scene, and there doesn't seem to be any mention of the United States in end time Bible prophecy, we must be a long way from the Tribulation and the Lord's return."

This is a more astute observation, and therefore it is more difficult to answer. Think of it — the signs of the times clearly indicate there is very little time left before the Tribulation and the Lord's return; yet, the world dominance of the United States does not jive with what the Bible seems to say will be the end time pattern of world politics.

Is the United States going to be suddenly removed from the world scene? Do we need to take another look at Bible prophecy to see if we have missed some important passages that might be speaking of America? What about Revelation 18? It speaks of a super power that dominates the world in the end times and which will be destroyed near the end of the Tribulation in one hour of one day (Revelation 18:8,10). Could this be the United States?

The Key Nation

Before we consider these important questions, let's take a look at the centerpiece of end time Bible prophecy regarding the nations. It is the nation of Israel. Over and over the Hebrew prophets prophesied that there would be a great end time regathering of the Jewish people that would result in the re-establishment of the nation of Israel. In fact, this is the most prolific prophecy in the Old Testament Scriptures, mentioned more than any other event.

A good example is to be found in Isaiah 11:10-12 —

> 10 Then it will come about in that day
> That the nations will resort to the root of Jesse,
> Who will stand as a signal for the peoples;
> And His resting place will be glorious.

> 11 Then it will happen on that day that the Lord
> Will again recover the second time with His hand
> The remnant of His people, who will remain,
> From Assyria, Egypt, Pathros, Cush, Elam,
> Shinar, Hamath,
> And from the islands of the sea.

> 12 And He will lift up a standard for the nations
> And will assemble the banished ones of Israel,
> And will gather the dispersed of Judah
> From the four corners of the earth.

I discovered this important passage, together with others like it, when I was a teenager. I took it to my pastor and asked him what it meant. He gave me the typical Amillennial answer, grounded in a belief that God has no purpose left for the Jewish people. He told me that it was a prophecy about the return of the Jewish people from Babylonian captivity. "It has already been fulfilled," he assured me. "It has nothing to do with the future."

Sleuthing Isaiah's Prophecy

Well, he couldn't have been more mistaken. Verse 11 specifically states that the prophecy is talking about a "second" regathering. The first was from Babylon. The second will be worldwide, and that is precisely what the prophecy asserts. It says the people will come from Assyria, Egypt, Pathros, Cush, Elam, Shinar [Babylon], and Hamath. The first regathering came only from Babylon. This second one will include Babylon, along with many other nations.

The prophecy could not be any clearer about this fact. It adds that the people will come "from the islands of the sea," which is a Hebrew colloquialism for the whole world. This point is re-emphasized in verse 12 where it states point blank that those regathered will come from "the four corners of the earth."

There is another clue that this prophecy is not talking about the return from Babylon. Verse 12 says that the regathered people will include "the banished ones of Israel" and "the dispersed of Judah." Those who returned from Babylon were captives from Judah. They did not include the people of the northern kingdom of Israel who had been captured and dispersed 200 years earlier by the Assyrians. The regathering described in Isaiah 11 will include Jews from both Israel and Judah.

The third clue that the passage has nothing to do with the return from Babylon is found in verse 10. Isaiah says this prophecy will be fulfilled "in that day." This is his standard term for the end times which he uses over and over again, for a total of 40 times (see for example, Isaiah 2:11, 10:20, and 28:5).

Verse 10 also says the prophecy will be fulfilled in a time when a "signal" is raised for the Jewish people — a signal that contains "the root of Jesse." The word translated "signal" also means flag, banner or pennant. The flag adopted for the modern state of Israel displays the star of David, the son of Jesse. The star of David was not used in biblical times as a symbol of the Jewish people.

Other Regathering Prophecies

A similar prophecy is contained in Zechariah 10 where the prophet records a promise of God:

> 6 "I will strengthen the house of Judah,
> And I will save the house of Joseph,
> And I will bring them back,

Because I have had compassion on them;
And they will be as though I had not
   rejected them . . .

9 "When I scatter them among the peoples,
They will remember Me in far countries,
And they with their children will live
   and come back."

Notice that verse 6 speaks of a great regathering of both Judah and "the house of Joseph," another term for the northern tribes of Israel. And verse 9 says they will come from "far countries." The special significance of this regathering prophecy is that it was written *after* the return from Babylon. It is, therefore, clearly pointing to a future regathering of all the Jewish people.

Another of the great end time regathering prophecies is found in Ezekiel 37. It is the famous prophecy of the valley of the dry bones. Ezekiel was brought by the Spirit of God to a valley strewn with bones. He was told to preach to the bones. (I've preached to some congregations like that, made up of the "frozen chosen.")

As Ezekiel began preaching, the bones began to come to life! They came back together, and muscles formed on them. As they resumed their human forms, breath came into them, and they stood up!

The astonished prophet was told by the Lord that the bones represented the Jewish people who had been scattered and seemed to have no hope. The Lord then assured Ezekiel that one day the "graves" of the Jewish people — the nations where they would be dispersed — would be opened, and the people would be brought back to the land of Israel (Ezekiel 37:11-12).

Again, Ezekiel asserts that this will be a regathering that will include both Israel and Judah: "Thus says the Lord God, 'Behold, I will take the stick of Joseph, which is in the hand of

Ephraim, and the tribes of Israel, his companions; and I will put them with it, with the stick of Judah, and make them one stick, and they will be one in My hand'" (Ezekiel 37:19). He also says this will occur right before the return of the Messiah to reign over the nations from Jerusalem (Ezekiel 37:24-28).

Triggering the Prophecies

The Lord launched His fulfillment of these prophecies near the end of the 19th Century when He gave a Viennese journalist a vision for the re-establishment of the state of Israel. The man was an Hungarian Jew by the name of Theodor Herzl (1860-1904). Like most Jewish intellectuals of his time, Herzl believed that the Jews had been assimilated into European society. But in 1894 his attitude radically changed.

He went to Paris to cover the trial of a French army officer by the name of Alfred Dreyfus. The officer had been falsely accused of treason because he was Jewish. When Herzl arrived at the court house, he was astonished to see thousands of Parisians standing in the streets shouting, "Death to the Jews!"

This agonizing experience convinced Herzl that the only hope for the Jews was for them to form a state of their own. He expressed this sentiment very convincingly in 1896 in a pamphlet called, "Der Judenstaat" ("The Jewish State"). His pamphlet led to the convocation of the First Zionist Congress, held in Basel, Switzerland in August of 1897. Herzl wrote in his diary, "At Basel, I founded the Jewish state." He predicted that within 50 years people would see the truth of his statement.

Sure enough, 50 years later in November 1947 the United Nations authorized the creation of a Jewish state in Palestine. And on May 14, 1948 the state of Israel came into existence.

Steps toward Statehood

At the beginning of the 20th Century, there were only 40,000 Jews in the land that the world called Palestine. In response to the urging of the World Zionist Organization, waves of Jewish immigrants began to return to Palestine where they bought land from the Arabs and established collective farms called *kibbutzim.*

The Zionist vision of re-establishing the state of Israel was endorsed by England in November of 1917 when the British government issued the Balfour Declaration. This important document was a product of the politics of World War I.

During that war, the Turkish Empire sided with the Germans. By late 1917 it was obvious that the Western Allies were going to defeat the Germans and the Turks. In anticipation of that victory, the Allies began to make plans for dividing up the German and Turkish empires. Britain was designated to receive Palestine as a League of Nations Mandate, meaning the British would be responsible for tutoring the people of Palestine toward self-government.

In the Balfour Declaration (named for the British Foreign Secretary, Arthur James Balfour), the British government declared its intention "to establish in Palestine . . . a national home for the Jewish people."

The British were to waffle on this commitment in the years to follow, particularly after the Arabs launched an intifada (uprising) in protest. In 1922, in an attempt to placate the Arabs, the British converted two-thirds of Palestine into the state of Jordan, leaving only a small sliver of land for the Jews on the west side of the Jordan River.

By the end of World War II there were almost 800,000 Jews in Palestine, most of them refugees who had fled from the Nazi Holocaust. There would have been many more if it had not been for British efforts during the war to curtail Jewish immigration.

In November 1947, as I pointed out before, the United Nations voted to allow the creation of the state of Israel. That was the good news for the Jews. The bad news was that the UN decided to divide the remaining sliver of land called Palestine between the Jews and the Arabs, producing a crazy quilt-work pattern of pieces to go to the Jews, with the Arabs getting the rest. The Jewish leaders were severely disappointed, but they accepted the decision and proclaimed their state on May 14, 1948. The Arabs rejected the UN decision and launched an all-out war against the new Jewish state, determined to annihilate it.

Since that time, the Arabs have fought six more wars with Israel: the Suez War of 1956, the Six Day War of 1967, the Yom Kippur War of 1973, the Lebanese War in 1982, the Gulf War in 1991, and the Arab Intifada which began in 2000. Despite having a great preponderance of power, the Arabs have lost all these wars. The miraculous survival of Israel is a fulfillment of a prophecy in Amos 9:15 where the Lord says that when the Jews are once more planted in their land, "they will not again be rooted out."

The Importance of Jerusalem

During the Six Day War in 1967 the Jews reconquered the city of Jerusalem which they had been unable to hold during their War of Independence (1948-1949). This occurred on June 7, 1967. It was a momentous event because it was the first time the Jews had exercised true sovereignty over their capital city since 70 AD — a span of 1,897 years.

In His Olivet discourse, given during the last week of His life, Jesus said to watch the city of Jerusalem. He prophesied that the city would fall by the sword, which it did 40 years later when the Romans destroyed it in 70 AD. He also prophesied that the city would be trampled down by the Gentiles "until the times of the Gentiles are fulfilled" (Luke 21:24). The Romans were followed by the Arabs (640-090), and then came the Crusaders (1090-1291), the Mamelukes

(1291-1517), the Turks (1517-1918), the League of Nations (1918-1922), the British (1922-1948), and the Jordanians (1948-1967).

The trampling down of Jerusalem by the Gentiles has not yet finished, for Jerusalem will be a battleground during the Tribulation, but the re-occupation of the city by the Jews is prophetically significant. The reason is that end time prophecies always portray the Jews back in their land and in their beloved city of Jerusalem. (See, for example, Zechariah 12:1-6.)

A Great Miracle

Today, [2003] there are 5.2 million Jews in Israel out of a total population of 13 million worldwide. They have come from over 100 countries in the greatest mass migration in human history. And they continue to come because, as the Scriptures state, God has put the road to Zion in their hearts (Psalm 84:5). For over three thousand years they have been ending every Passover meal with the prayer, "Next year in Jerusalem!" God has finally activated the instinct of their hearts, and like homing pigeons, they are streaming home.

Jeremiah makes an astounding observation about this regathering in Jeremiah 16:14-15. He says that when God has completed His purposes for the Jews, they will look back on their history and consider their regathering from all over the world to be a greater miracle than their deliverance from Egyptian captivity!

> 14 "Therefore, behold, days are coming," declares the Lord, "when it will no longer be said, 'As the Lord lives, who brought up the sons of Israel out of the land of Egypt,'
>
> 15 but, 'As the Lord lives, who brought up the sons of Israel from the land of the north and from all the countries where

He had banished them.' For I will restore
them to their own land which I gave to
their fathers."

Against all odds, God has accomplished the impossible by preserving the Jewish people, restoring them to their land, and enabling them to re-establish their state.

And so, the key piece of the end time pattern of nations is in place — the nation of Israel exists again. The rest of the pattern revolves around Israel.

The Arab Threat

Once Israel is re-established, as it has been, the Bible prophesies that it will be threatened from all sides by a variety of nations. First and foremost, the very existence of Israel will be challenged by the surrounding Arab states.

Ezekiel prophesied that "at the time of the punishment of the end" (his term for the end times), God will pour out His wrath upon "Mount Seir" (his collective term for the Arab peoples) because they will covet the land which He has given the Jews (Ezekiel 35:5,10-11). Isaiah had previously given the same prophecy when he stated that a time will come when God will pour out His wrath upon Edom (Isaiah's collective term for the Arabs) because of their mistreatment of the Jewish people (Isaiah 34:5-6).

The end time Arab conspiracy to destroy Israel is spelled out in detail in Psalm 83 where the psalmist says that the Arab nations of Jordan, Egypt, Lebanon, Gaza, Saudi Arabia, and Syria will make a covenant to "possess for ourselves the pastures of God [the land of Israel]" (Psalm 83:5-12).

These prophecies have been partially fulfilled since the re-establishment of the Jewish state in 1948. The Arab nations surrounding Israel have launched six wars in a never-ceasing attempt to annihilate the Jewish state. Additionally, there have been several significant intifadas (Palestinian uprisings), climaxing with the one that began in September 2000.

The Oslo Process

The current "land for peace" process that was inaugurated by the Oslo Accords of 1993 was a sham from the beginning. Yassar Arafat made this crystal clear in the speeches he gave in Arabic immediately following the ceremonies conducted at the White House in September 1993.

In response to his Arab critics who accused him of selling out to the Israelis, he kept reminding the Arab world of Mohammad's Treaty of Qurish. This was a treaty of peace that Mohammad made with a Saudi Arabian tribe that refused to convert to Islam. As soon as he accumulated sufficient power, he tossed the treaty aside and forcibly subdued the tribe. In other words, Arafat was assuring the Arab world that the Oslo Accords were a temporary measure designed to give him a toe-hold of territory in Israel from which he would launch the final assault on the Israelis as soon as he had sufficient power.

Arafat had already spelled out this strategy in detail long before in 1974 when his PLO terrorist organization issued what it called, "The Phased Plan." This plan recognized the impossibility of defeating Israel militarily. It called instead for a diplomatic defeat by rallying the United States, Western Europe, and the United Nations to put pressure on Israel to trade land for peace. In short, it was a trojan horse strategy. The Arabs, pretending to desire peace, would use world diplomatic pressure to force Israel to cede parcels of land from which the final assault would ultimately be launched.

The process was birthed in 1991 when the Soviet Union collapsed and Israel was flooded with Jewish immigrants, arriving at the rate of 2,000 to 3,000 a day. In one year's time, Israel received a number of immigrants equivalent to the United States absorbing the entire population of France! Israel was literally overwhelmed. The nation desperately needed financial help. The Israelis turned to their best friend, the

United States, and asked us to guarantee a $5 billion loan from the World Bank. The Bush Administration agreed to do so only if the Israelis would start negotiating with the Palestinians, offering to trade land for peace.

Yes, the United States is the one who forced the Israelis to begin the suicidal process of offering land for peace. It triggered the PLO's "Phased Plan." It was a process doomed to failure, for history proves that appeasement never leads to peace. Instead, it merely serves to whet the appetite of the aggressor.

The Russian Threat

The Arabs are not the only enemies of Israel prophesied for the end times. The Bible says another nemesis of the Jews will be Russia. In Ezekiel 38 and 39 we are told that a nation from "the remote parts of the north" will prove to be Israel's greatest enemy (Ezekiel 38:6,15).

All directions in the Bible are given in reference to Jerusalem. If you take a string and put one end of it on the city Jerusalem on a world globe and then place the other end on the North Pole, you will see that the string passes through Moscow, the capital of Russia. This is a good indication that Ezekiel is speaking of Russia as the nation in "the remote parts of the north."

There are other indicators. Ezekiel says this nation will comprise the land of Magog (Ezekiel 38:2), which Josephus identified as the area occupied by the Scythians in south central Russia. It is also identified as the land ruled by "the prince of Rosh" (Ezekiel 38:2). Rosh is an ancient root word for Russia. The ruler is also identified as being in control of Meshech and Tubal — possibly ancient names for Moscow and Tobolsk.

The Russians are pictured as invading Israel with a coalition of nations. Persia is named first (Ezekiel 38:5). At that time, Persia included modern day Syria, Iraq, Iran, and

Afghanistan. Named also are Ethiopia, Put (Libya), and two areas — Gomer and Beth-togarmah — included in modern day Turkey (Ezekiel 38:5-6).

Ezekiel says the Russian invasion of Israel will occur at a time when the Jews are living in unwalled cities, as is the case today (Ezekiel 38:11). He also says the purpose of the invasion will be "to capture spoil and to seize plunder" (Ezekiel 38:12). We will see later what this could be referring to.

As I stated earlier in this chapter, there is no nation on earth with a longer and more persistent anti-Semitic history than Russia. Russian rulers have used the Jews as their whipping boys throughout their recorded history, blaming all the ills of Russian society on "the international Jewish conspiracy." That demonic spirit of anti-Semitism remains firmly rooted in Russian society to this day.

The Role of Europe

Europe is another big-time player in the Bible's end time scenario of events. The prophecies contained in Daniel and Revelation make it clear that in the end times, the Roman Empire will be revived and, out of it, the Antichrist will arise.

Nebuchadnezzer's dream, which we discussed in chapter 1, revealed a progression of future Gentile empires: Babylon, Medo-Persia, Greece, and Rome (Daniel 2:31-45). It also revealed that the final Gentile empire would be related to the Roman Empire and would consist of a loose confederation of ten nations or regions.

Daniel's vision of the same procession of empires, given to him 48 years later, also indicated the last Gentile empire of history would be a confederation of ten units that would be located in the area of the old Roman Empire (Daniel 7:1-8). Further, Daniel was shown that the Antichrist would rise out of this reconstructed Roman Empire, first taking over three of the units, and then the rest (Daniel 7:8-12, 23-26).

In chapter 9 of his prophecies, Daniel again asserts that the Antichrist will rise out of a revised Roman Empire. He states that the Antichrist will originate from among the people who would one day destroy the Jewish temple (Daniel 9:26). Those people proved, of course, to be the Romans in 70 AD.

New Testament Confirmation

The apostle John confirmed the message of Daniel's visions in the book of Revelation. In chapter 17 he sees a "woman sitting on a scarlet beast . . . having seven heads and ten horns" (Revelation 17:3). We know the beast is Satan because he is described with the same terminology in Revelation 12:3. The woman is symbolic of the apostate church which the Antichrist will use to inspire worldwide worship of himself (Revelation 13:12).

John explains that the seven heads of the beast represent "seven kings," five which had already fallen, one which existed at that time, and the seventh which is yet to come (Revelation 17:10). This appears to be a reference to a succession of Gentile world empires. The five fallen would be Egypt, Assyria, Babylon, Medo-Persia, and Greece. The one existing at that time was Rome. The one yet to come would be the end time European confederation, representing a revival of the Roman Empire. John then reveals that the revived Roman Empire will evolve into the eighth and final Gentile empire of history — namely, the worldwide empire of the Antichrist (Revelation 17:11-12).

A Persistent Dream

It is interesting to note that ever since the Roman Empire ceased to exist in 476 AD, repeated attempts have been made throughout history to revive it. In the Middle Ages the Pope attempted a revival through the creation of what was called the Holy Roman Empire. But it was an empire in name only. Napoleon and Hitler both tried to unite Europe through military power, and both failed because it was not God's timing.

Undoubtedly, all these attempts were inspired by Satan. He knows Bible prophecy (Revelation 12:12), and he therefore understands that he cannot raise up his false messiah, the Antichrist, until he is able to orchestrate the reunification of Europe.

The Impact of World War II

The turning point for the fulfillment of these prophecies came with World War II. Just as the War accelerated the re-establishment of Israel by motivating the Jewish people to go back home, it also motivated the movement toward European unity.

When the war ended, Europe was in ruins and was desperate. This desperation prompted European leaders to put aside ancient hatreds and jealousies in order to reach out to each other for mutual support and aid.

The result was a series of economic mergers which were ultimately to lead to political integration. It all began a little over 50 years ago on May 9, 1950 when the French foreign minister, Robert Schuman, announced a plan conceived by a French businessman, Jean Monnet.

The plan was to pool European coal and steel production. The result was the formation in 1951 of the European Coal and Steel Community, consisting of France, Germany, Italy, the Netherlands, Belgium, and Luxembourg. This cooperative venture proved so successful that the member states decided to expand its scope to include all aspects of their economies.

From Economic to Political Union

The step toward economic union was taken in March of 1957 with the signing of the Treaty of Rome. The members of the European Coal and Steel Community agreed to set up a Common Market which went into effect in January 1958. This resulted in the economic integration and unification of the economies of the participating nations.

The next step came in 1973 when three nations were added to the European Economic Community. They were Denmark, Ireland, and Britain. Later additions included Greece in 1981, Spain and Portugal in 1986, and Austria, Finland and Sweden in 1995. These additions brought the total membership to 15 nations.

The culminating step took place in February 1992 when the Maastricht Treaty was signed that transformed the European Economic Community into a political and economic entity called the European Union — a Union that came into existence in 1993.

The Emergence of a Super State

Since that time, the European Union has rapidly evolved into a super state.

It is hard for most people to believe the degree of sovereignty that has already been surrendered by the member states. For example, the chief legislative body of the EU, located in Brussels, Belgium and called the Council of Europe, has the power to overrule all national laws of member states. Likewise, the European Court of Justice in Luxembourg has the power to override the decisions made by the supreme courts of the member states.

At the present time [2003] there is a collective executive branch called the European Commission. It is also headquartered in Brussels. It consists of 20 members appointed by the member states for terms of 5 years. This group selects the chief administrative officer of the European Union, called the president of the Commission. This person is the CEO of the EU. This is the position the future Antichrist could likely control.

The most interesting organization within the EU is the European Parliament, located in Strasbourg, France. It consists of 626 members [2003] who are directly elected by regions for 5 year terms. The name of this group is confusing because you would think it is the chief legislative body. But it is not. The Council is the legislative body.

Currently [2003], the European Parliament is a parliament in name only. Mainly, it is a public forum — a sort of European town hall. But its voice carries a lot of weight. Most legislative proposals originate from its deliberations, and it is growing in power, emerging as the lower house of what is likely to become a two house parliament — with the Council serving as the upper house, or the Senate.

Members of the European Parliament sit in political blocs according to ideology, and not nationalities. This is part of a concerted effort to break down national allegiances.

Financial Aspects

The financial branch of the EU governmental structure is called The European Central Bank. It is located in Frankfurt, Germany. This bank introduced a new currency in 1999 called the Euro. In January 2002 that currency replaced the national currencies of all the members states except Denmark, Sweden, and England. That means there is no longer a German Mark, or an Italian Lira, or a French Franc. The British are trying to retain the English Pound, but it appears to be doomed.

Revenue for the EU is generated by a 1.27% tax of each nation's gross national income. Revenue is also derived from a VAT tax and custom duties. In 2000, the income totaled $93 billion.

The Missing Element

As you can see, the European Union has all the trappings of a state — governmental agencies (legislative, executive and judicial), taxing power, and a common currency.

One of the main things missing has been a police force. But it is forming. The European Union is currently putting together an army of 60,000 called "the rapid-action Eurocorps."

A Revived Empire

A new European holiday has been created — May 9th — to celebrate the building of this new European empire. And the statistics make it clear that we are truly talking about a new world empire.

The 15 member nations consist of 374 million people and their combined economies constitute 20% of the world's gross domestic product and 20% of world trade. In comparison to the United States and Japan, the European Union excels both in population and in world trade.

Significantly, the European Union is poised for a major expansion. The treaty of Nice, negotiated in December 2000, provides for the admission of Cypress and Malta, plus eight former Communist countries in Eastern Europe: Latvia, Lithuania, Estonia, Poland, Hungary, the Czech Republic, Slovakia, and Slovenia. The treaty was ratified in October 2002, and the ten new states are scheduled to be added to the Union in January of 2004.

When these are added, the European Union will consist of 25 nations representing nearly 500 million people! Their combined economies will constitute 31% of the world's gross domestic product and 30% of world trade. Agin, in comparison to the United States and Japan, the expanded European Union will excel both in population, gross domestic product, and world trade.

The main thing this super state now lacks is a super leader. The attitude exists for the emergence of such a person. One of the early leaders toward European unity was Paul Henri Spaak of Belgium. Fifty years ago he said, "We do not want another committee . . . What we want is a man of sufficient stature to hold the allegiance of all the people . . . Send us such a man and, be he God or the devil, we will receive him."

Spiritual Implications

There are many spiritual implications of the European Union — factors which make it clear that Satan must be the motivating force behind the whole movement. Consider, for example, the Tower of Babel motif which the EU frequently uses in its advertising, together with the slogan, "Many tongues, one voice." It is astonishing that a symbol which spiritually represents Man's rebellion against God has been selected to serve as one of the identifying themes of the European Union.

The fascination with this demonic symbol resulted in the parliament building in Strasbourg, France being designed to look like artist's renditions of the ancient tower of Babel! It is as if all of Europe is saying that they will succeed where Babylon failed by uniting Mankind against God and reversing God's judgment of converting one voice into many languages.

Catholic Influence

There is a spiritual theme incorporated into the EU Flag that is taken from Catholic doctrine. The flag features 12 gold stars in a circle on a blue background. Why 12 when there are 25 members states? It's because the symbolism is taken from the Catholic Church's traditional portrayal of Mary with a halo of 12 stars. The church's imagery is drawn from Revelation 12 where a woman appears with a halo of 12 stars. This imagery is drawn directly from Joseph's dream in the Old Testament, and the image represents Israel, not Mary.

A former Secretary General of the Council of Europe, Leon Marchal, affirmed that the stars on the EU flag are those of "the woman of the Apocalypse." Enthusiastically, he explained, "It's wonderful that we have gotten back to the Introit of the new Mass of the Assumption. The symbol is the *corona stellarum duodecim* (the crown of the twelve stars) of the woman of the Apocalypse."

It is no wonder that Vatican authorities have enthusiastically endorsed the European Union from its inception.

More Demonic Symbolism

The EU Anthem is "Ode to Joy," the prelude of the last movement of Beethoven's Ninth Symphony. Appropriately, the words, by Fredrich von Schiller, concern Mankind entering the shrine of a pagan goddess who unites all Men by the power of magic.

The EU Logo is, incredibly, a woman riding on a beast! It comes right out of the Satanic imagery of Revelation 17 where a harlot is portrayed riding on a beast in the sea. This woman represents the apostate religion of the Antichrist.

The Europeans don't see it that way. They view it as a representation of an ancient myth about a woman named Europa who was captured and raped by the god Zeus who disguised himself as a bull. But even so, why would anyone want to use such a pagan, repulsive story as the symbol of a new super state?

This symbol can be found in a mammoth painting in the EU Parliament's new building in Brussels. It is also featured in a huge sculpture located in the courtyard of the Council of Ministers office in Brussels. The symbol is portrayed on several of the Euro coins and stamps and is being used widely on items like telephone cards and credit cards. To the modern European mind, this symbol represents the taming of the beast of nationalism through European unity.

Fulfilled Prophecy

The end time super state prophesied by Daniel has been born. The Roman Empire is being revived. It is being resurrected from the dead before our very eyes. It will soon give birth to the Antichrist who will use it as his base to conquer the world.

Every possible effort is being made to replace national identities with a common European identity. The EU flag has replaced national flags on driver's licenses and auto license plates. Passports now identify the carriers primarily as citizens of the European Union. Members of the European Parliament are elected from regions, not from nations, and they are not allowed to sit in the parliament by national groupings. It is probably only a matter of time before the EU will suppress national identities even further by dividing all of Europe into ten administrative units.

A former colleague of mine, Dennis Pollock, shared with me an insight of his regarding the European Union: "The first time Jesus came, the Roman Empire controlled the world and Israel existed as a nation within that empire. The Romans and Jews conspired together to murder Jesus. When Jesus returns, the Roman Empire will control the world again and Israel will once again be part of it. But this time, the Jews will reject Rome, a great remnant will be saved, and Jesus will destroy the Revived Roman Empire."

We are living in exciting times when we can see prophecy fulfilled before our very eyes. The revival of the Roman Empire is one of those fulfillments, and it is a sure sign that we are living on borrowed time.

The Likely Scenario

Now that the prophesied end time pattern of world politics is in place for the first time, what is likely to be the outcome of international politics?

The Bible says that as we approach the threshold of the Tribulation, leading up to the day of the Lord's return, the world will become increasingly hostile to Israel. In fact, we are told that the whole world will come together against Israel over the issue of Jerusalem (Zechariah 12:2-3).

That is precisely where we are today in the end time scenario of events. The Arab nations are demanding sovereignty over Jerusalem. The European Union is insisting that the city be divided between the Arabs and the Jews. The United Nations would like to see the city internationalized, and the Vatican would like to see it put under its control. Even Israel's greatest ally, the United States, is pressuring the Jews to surrender a part of the city.

A War for Jerusalem

All of this international pressure is leading up to a major conflagration over the control of the city. When the war breaks out, the Israelis will win it quickly, prompting the Palestinians to send out a call for help to the Arab world. The Syrians are most likely the ones who will jump in first, due to their implacable hatred of the Jews. They will target both Tel Aviv and Haifa with missiles, and the only way Israel will be able to survive is to retaliate with its own missiles, possibly using nuclear warheads. This would explain the fact that Bible prophecy clearly states that Damascus, the capital of Syria, will cease to exist in the end times (Isaiah 17:1-14 and Jeremiah 49:23-27).

The whole Arab world will be thrown into a panic over the destruction of Damascus, and the Arab leaders will turn to their natural ally for help — Russia. The Russians will respond gleefully to the Arab invitation because they will see it as an opportunity not only to destroy Israel, but to seize the oil fields of the Middle East. This is most likely the "plunder" that will draw them into the area (Ezekiel 38:12).

The Russian troops will be destroyed supernaturally on the hills of Israel. It will happen in such a way that even the Israelis will realize that the defeat came from God, and many Jewish hearts will be turned to the Lord (Ezekiel 39:1-6).

The Rise of the Antichrist

At this point the whole world will be thrown into a panic, and into that atmosphere will step a dynamic, charismatic political leader from Europe who will seem to have all the answers. He will broker an amazing settlement for the Middle East that will enable the Jews to truly live in peace and even to rebuild their temple.

He will use his success in the Middle East to take over the European Union, and he will use that empire as his base for launching a war to take over the world. He will be spectacularly successful, due to his ruthlessness. He will slaughter one-half of the world's population in a nuclear war that will enable him to become the first person in history to conquer all the nations of the world. He will combine them into the final Gentile empire of history which he will rule from Rome (Daniel 7:23-26, Daniel 8:23-26, and Revelation 6-9).

The Nagging Question

All of which brings us full circle to the question we started off with: Where is the United States in these end time events? What role will we play? And if the Bible is silent about us, how is that to be explained? After all, we are the nation that dominates world politics at the very time when all the signs of the time point to a quick fulfillment of these end time prophecies.

Chapter 3

The Search for America:
Are we missing in action?

"Blessed is the nation whose God is the Lord."
Psalm 33:12

Several years ago I got a call from a friend who was a student of Bible prophecy. When I answered, he shouted triumphantly, " I have discovered America!"

I thought for a moment and then replied, " I thought Columbus did that!"

"No," he shot back, "I mean I have discovered America in Bible prophecy." He proceeded to explain how he had concluded that the United States must be the super power described in Revelation 18 — the power that dominates the world during the Tribulation.

An Understandable Quest

It is only natural that we should wonder where the United States is in Bible prophecy. We love our nation. We are concerned about its future. And we are mystified by the fact that it does not seem to be specifically mentioned in God's Prophetic Word.

The persistent question about America's future has motivated many prophecy experts to resort to their imaginations. The unfortunate result has been the "discovery" of the United States in some very unusual passages — passages that strain credulity. This imaginative approach to the interpretation of Bible prophecy is one of several factors that have motivated contempt for the whole field of prophetic studies, prompting many people to write it off as "a playground for fanatics."

Let's take a look at some of these passages of Scripture where the United States has been "found," and let's try to determine whether or not the discovery has really been made.

A "tall and smooth people"?

1 Alas, oh land of whirring wings
Which lies beyond the rivers of Cush,

2 Which sends envoys by the sea . . .
Go, swift messengers, to a nation tall and smooth,
To a people feared far and wide,
A powerful and oppressive nation
Whose land the rivers divide . . .

7 At that time a gift of homage will be brought to the Lord of hosts
From a people tall and smooth,
Even from a people feared far and wide,
A powerful and oppressive nation,
Whose land the rivers divide —
To the place of the name of the Lord of hosts, even Mount Zion.

Some have used these verses from Isaiah 18 to prove that the United States is in Bible prophecy. They note that the passage speaks of a people "tall and smooth" who are "feared far and wide" (verse 2). The passage further states that this is a "powerful nation whose land the rivers divide" (verse 2). The chapter ends by stating that the people of this nation will bring "a gift of homage" to the Lord when He returns to reign from Mt. Zion (verse 7).

Because these verses speak of a powerful nation whose land is divided by a great river, some people with rather vivid imaginations have jumped to the conclusion that the nation is the United States, since it is divided by the Mississippi River. They further argue that we are a people who are tall and clean-shaven, and that our military might is feared throughout the world. Finally, they argue that since we are a Christian nation, we would certainly bring gifts to the Lord when He returns.

But the opening verse of this chapter states specifically that it is speaking of the nation of "Cush," the ancient name of Ethiopia. At the time Isaiah wrote this passage, Ethiopia was the seat of the powerful 25th Egyptian Dynasty (730-660 BC). The river referred to is undoubtedly the Nile.

The prophecy that the Egyptians will pay homage to the Lord during His future reign over all the earth is explained in detail in the next chapter. In Isaiah 19:16-25, Isaiah reveals that when the Lord returns, He "will make Himself known to Egypt, and the Egyptians will know the Lord in that day. They will even worship with sacrifice and offering, and will make a vow to the Lord and perform it" (verse 21).

Isaiah proceeds to explain that a highway will be built that will connect the old foes of the Middle East — Syria, Israel and Egypt. The three will be united by a common faith in the same Lord, and their people will move freely along this highway from one country to the other (Isaiah 19:23-25).

The three nations will live in peace and harmony and will be considered "a blessing in the midst of the earth" (verse 24). In fact, the Lord Himself will proclaim: "Blessed is Egypt My people, and Assyria the work of My hands, and Israel My inheritance" (verse 25).

Isaiah 18 has nothing to do with the United States in prophecy, and even if it did, it would not answer the question about the role of America in end time world politics. It is a prophecy about the millennial reign of Jesus that will be established after His return.

A "village" of Tarshish?

Probably one of the most popular passages where people claim to have found America is in Ezekiel 38 where the prophet describes an invasion of Israel that will be launched in the end times by a nation "from the remote parts of the north" (verse 15). The descriptive verses about the northern power make it clear that this nation is Russia. What is not so clear is where the United States fits into this invasion.

Those who find us in the passage point to Ezekiel 38:13 which says that "the merchants of Tarshish and all its villages" (or "young lions," depending on the translation) will speak out against the invasion. The argument is that Tarshish is Britain and the "villages," or "young lions," are the English speaking nations like the United States and Australia that were founded by British immigrants.

To say the least, this is a highly imaginative interpretation. It truly shows the desperation that people feel in trying to find America in prophecy. Those who cling to this passage end up building an upside down pyramid, with a major conclusion resting on the tip of one very obtuse verse.

The validity of the argument is seriously questioned by the fact that no one knows for certain the true identity of "Tarshish." In recent years the interpretation has fallen on hard times because archaeological discoveries indicate that Tarshish was most likely ancient Tartessus in modern day Spain.

But the diehards have continued to cling to Ezekiel 38 as the passage that refers to the United States in prophecy. They have responded to the archaeological evidence by saying, "It makes no difference if Tarshish really is Spain. After all, who discovered America? Columbus. And where did he come from? Spain!" So, their new interpretation is that the "merchants of Tarshish" are all the nations of the world that were developed from Spanish explorations. These mental gymnastics show how hard it is to give up old theories in the light of new evidence.

Tarshish is used in Scripture as a symbol of the areas west of Israel. Therefore, the most likely meaning of Ezekiel's statement is that the nations of Western Europe will speak out against the Russian-led invasion of Israel in the end times.

One thing is certain — Ezekiel 38 does not settle the search for America in prophecy.

A "great eagle"?

Sometimes the search for the United States in prophecy becomes downright silly. For example, another favorite passage for applied imagination is found in Revelation 12:13-14 —

> 13 And when the dragon saw that he was thrown down to earth, he persecuted the woman who gave birth to the male child.
>
> 14 And the two wings of the great eagle were given to the woman, so that she could fly into the wilderness to her place, where she was nourished for a time and times and half a time, from the presence of the serpent.

The "woman who gave birth to the male child" (verse 13) is Israel. So, these verses are saying that in the middle of the Tribulation God will provide a means of escape for the Jewish remnant in Israel. They will be carried into the wilderness to a hiding place on the "wings of a great eagle" (verse 14).

Some people have seized on this imagery to teach that the United States, whose national symbol is the eagle, will supply the end time air lift that will save the Jewish remnant!

But the Bible is its own best interpreter. And when you look up the phrase, "wings of an eagle," you will find that it is the same one that God used in Exodus 19:4 to describe how

He brought the Israelites out of Egypt: "You yourselves have seen what I did to the Egyptians, and how I bore you on eagles' wings, and brought you to Myself." The same imagery is used in Deuteronomy 32:11 where it speaks of God's protection of Israel in the wilderness: "Like an eagle that stirs up its nest, that hovers over its young, He [the Lord] spread His wings and caught them, He carried them on His pinions."

God is often portrayed in the Scriptures symbolically as a protective bird. In Psalm 91 the reader is told to put his trust in God and He will "cover you with His pinions, and under His wings you may seek refuge" (Psalm 91:2,4). In Psalm 17:8 David cries out to the Lord in a prayer, asking God to "hide me in the shadow of Your wings." (See also Psalms 36:7, 57:1, 61:4, and 63:7.)

In Revelation 12, God is the "eagle," not the United States. All the passage in Revelation 12 teaches is that God is going to supernaturally protect the Jewish people when they flee from the Antichrist into Jordan in the middle of the Tribulation.

"Babylon the great"?

This brings us to the final and most widely used passage for identifying the United States in Bible prophecy. It is Revelation 18 where the destruction of "Babylon the great" is described:

> 1 After these things I saw another angel coming down from heaven, having great authority . . .

> 2 And he cried out with a mighty voice, saying, "Fallen, fallen is Babylon the great! She has become a dwelling place of demons and a prison of every unclean spirit, and a prison of every unclean and hateful bird.

> 3 For all the nations have drunk of the wine of the passion of her immorality, and the kings of the earth have committed acts of immorality with her, and the merchants of the earth have become rich by the wealth of her sensuality . . .

> 8 For this reason in one day her plagues will come, pestilence and mourning and famine, and she will be burned up with fire; for the Lord God who judges her is strong.

> 9 And the kings of the earth, who committed acts of immorality and lived sensuously with her, will weep and lament over her when they see the smoke of her burning.

There is no doubt that the United States shares many similarities with the corrupt commercial empire described in this chapter. The empire is described as one that is in rebellion against God, to the point that it has become "a dwelling place of demons" (verse 2). It further states that the immorality of this empire has corrupted all the nations of the world (verse 3).

It is also made clear that this "Babylon the great" will completely dominate the world economy, and its destruction will result in the collapse of the economies of all nations. This causes the kings, merchants and shipmasters to "weep and lament" and cry out, "Woe, woe!" (verses 9,11,17).

In the present international context, it certainly sounds like the United States. But, again, the Bible is its own best interpreter, and chapter 17 of Revelation makes it clear that "Babylon the great" is an empire whose capital is Rome, not Washington, D.C.

The Scripture Context

In Revelation 17:9 we are told that the seven heads of the beast (the Antichrist) are representative, in part, of "seven mountains." In the First Century context, this could only be a reference to Rome, for it was known as "the city of seven hills." This identification is further reinforced by verse 18 which states that the woman riding the beast "is the great city, which reigns over the kings of the earth." Again, there is only one city that could fit that description in the First Century context of the passage, and that is Rome.

When Revelation 17 and 18 are considered in reference to what the rest of the book teaches about the events of the Tribulation, it is clear that the "Babylon the great" that is mentioned in these two chapters is the last Gentile world empire, the empire of the Antichrist.

The book of Daniel teaches that this empire will be centered in the geographical base of the old Roman empire, which, of course, is what we now refer to as Western Europe (Daniel 7). Revelation 17 and 18 reveal that the capital of this empire will be Rome. And Revelation 13:7 states that this empire will truly be worldwide in nature, encompassing every nation on the face of the earth: "And it was also given to him [the Antichrist] to make war with the saints and to overcome them; and authority over every tribe and people and tongue and nation was given to him."

Most Bible prophecies have a pre-fillment in symbolic type before they are ultimately fulfilled in reality. The destruction of the United States (whether by external or internal forces), and the impact of that destruction upon the world, could certainly constitute a pre-fillment of Revelation 17 and 18, but the true fulfillment will have to await the annihilation of the empire of the Antichrist.

Some Conclusions

So, where is the United States in Bible prophecy? A partial answer is that we are not mentioned directly and specifically. We are covered by general prophecies that relate to all nations, but beyond that, our end time destiny is not specifically mentioned.

General prophecies that apply to the United States include those that say all nations will be judged (Isaiah 34:2-3) and all nations will cease to exist except the nation of Israel (Jeremiah 30:11 and 46:28).

But how could God overlook the world's most important and powerful nation? I don't think He has. I believe America can be found in Bible prophecy, not specifically, but in prophetic type. In other words, I believe there is a nation in Scripture that is a forerunner of America in its origin, its purpose, and its destiny. Let's take a look at that nation.

Prophetic Types

But first, let me make certain that you understand the concept of a prophetic type. This term refers to a person, an object, a nation, or even an historical event that stands as a prophetic symbol of something yet to occur in history.

Joseph was a prophetic type of the Messiah. Like Jesus, he presented himself to his brethren with a special message from God, and he was rejected. He experienced a symbolic killing and resurrection when he was cast into a pit by his brothers and was later rescued by a passing caravan. He departed his homeland, just as Jesus departed this earth when He ascended into Heaven. Joseph then took a Gentile bride, just as Jesus is doing now, His bride being the Church. Then Joseph revealed himself to his brethren again, and they received him, even as a great remnant of the Jewish people will receive Jesus as Messiah when He returns.

Nehemiah appears to be a prophetic type of the Holy Spirit and the work He does in the life of the believer today. Like the Spirit, Nehemiah served as a source of inspiration, power, and guidance for his people as they rebuilt the walls of Jerusalem.

The kings of Babylon and Tyre are used in the Bible as symbols of Satan (Isaiah 14 and Ezekiel 28). They are also prophetic types of the Antichrist. The tyrant Antiochus Epiphanes is likewise presented as a type of the Antichrist in Daniel 11.

Sometimes inanimate objects are used as prophetic types — like the Ark of the Covenant and the Tabernacle of Moses. Almost every element of these structures pointed in some way to either a characteristic of the Messiah or some aspect of His work of salvation. Thus, the Ark was made of wood and overlaid with gold to signify that the Messiah would be both human and divine. The Ark contained three objects: Moses' tablets of stone, a bowl of manna, and Aaron's rod that budded. These signified that the Messiah would obey the Law perfectly, that He would be the bread of life, and that He would be resurrected from the dead.

Even historical events can serve as prophetic types. The nation of Israel was born in Canaan, exiled to Egypt, experienced the "baptism of Moses" when leaving Egypt, and then was tested in the wilderness for 40 years before entering the promised land. In like manner, Jesus was born in Canaan and then was taken to Egypt before being baptized by John the Baptist, after which He was tested in the wilderness for 40 days before entering into His ministry.

America's Prophetic Type

I believe the biblical prophetic type of the United States is the nation of Judah. This was the southern nation that was formed when the United Kingdom of David and Solomon broke up after Solomon's death.

The northern nation of Israel, consisting of ten tribes, was born in rebellion, and it was never blessed by God. Throughout its 208 year history it never had one king who was considered to be righteous in the eyes of God.

In stark contrast, the southern kingdom of Judah, which contained both the city of Jerusalem and the Jewish temple, was blessed like no other nation that had ever existed. The nation was given eight righteous kings during its 344 years of existence. The combined rule of those kings constituted 224 years of the nation's history. These included great men of God like Jehoshaphat, Hezekiah, and Josiah. This godly leadership produced a nation blessed with freedom, prosperity, justice and peace.

But the nation's greatest blessing was the presence of God Himself in the form of His Shekinah Glory which resided in the Temple's Holy of Holies.

The American Parallel

No other nation has since been so richly blessed except the United States of America. God gave us a great expanse of territory filled with every conceivable natural resource. Additionally, He gave us the ingenuity to harness our natural resources and talents to produce the greatest wealth the world has ever known.

Like ancient Judah, God blessed us with godly political leaders who loved Him and who cherished freedom. He also gave us great spiritual leaders who preached the Gospel with zeal and developed a citizenry grounded in Christian principles of justice and brotherhood.

And working through our wealth and churches, the Lord sent forth missionaries all over the world to establish churches and translate the Bible into many languages.

Never were truer words spoken about the heritage of America than those lines contained in the great song, "America the Beautiful:"

> America! America!
> God shed His grace on thee,
> And crown thy good
> With brotherhood
> From sea to shining sea.

It would be great if we could conclude our comparison of Judah and America at this point. But unfortunately, the parallels in the histories of the two nations do not end here.

Pride and Rebellion

When Judah reached the height of her glory as a nation, the people began to wallow in pride, and this led to rebellion against God and His Word. They had been warned about this in the writings of Moses as recorded in Deuteronomy 8:11,17:

> 11 Beware lest you forget the Lord your God by not keeping His commandments and His ordinances and His statutes which I am commanding you today;

> 17 Otherwise, you may say in your heart, "My power and the strength of my hand made me this wealth."

Often when I am asked, "Where is the United States in Bible Prophecy?" I respond by saying, "Look in Isaiah chapter 5. Or consider Jeremiah 5 and 6." I say that because these chapters contain an inventory of the national sins of Judah as catalogued by Isaiah and Jeremiah, and they are the same sins that characterize American society today.

Injustice and Greed

The first sin mentioned by Isaiah is injustice. He says he searched for justice but found, instead, "bloodshed" and "a cry of distress" (Isaiah 5:7).

In like manner, injustice is rampant in America today. Obtaining justice in our system too often depends on skin color, contacts, and money. Violence has grown exponentially, and our criminal justice system has become a revolving door due to an obsession with the protection of the rights of criminals.

The second sin Isaiah identifies is greed: "Woe to those who add house to house and join field to field, until there is no room" (Isaiah 5:8).

Greed is the controlling attitude in American society today. Big business wants more money for its products regardless of quality. Big labor wants more money for its workers regardless of productivity. Big sports continues to demand higher salaries despite obscenely high wage levels. Big government has an insatiable appetite for more taxes. And saddest of all, big religion begs for more donations, promising multiples in return, thus appealing to the greed of its donors.

Hedonism and Blasphemy

Isaiah focuses next on the sin of pleasure-seeking. He refers to "those who rise early in the morning that they may pursue strong drink" and those "who stay up late in the evening" to revel at parties while paying no attention to the Lord (Isaiah 5:11-12).

I don't think it is any exaggeration to say that like Judah, America has given its heart to hedonism. Our national motto could easily be, "If it feels good, do it!" This attitude is reflected in the advertising of products with slogans that emphasize "we only go around once," and we therefore need "to grab all the gusto" we can.

The next sin Isaiah condemns is blasphemy. He graphically describes how people flaunt their sins and then shake their fists at God, daring Him to do anything about their rebellious lifestyles (Isaiah 5:18-19).

I can remember when a Hollywood movie star had to flee the country in shame because it was revealed that she was living with a man she was not married to. Today, the stars appear on national television talk shows and openly brag about their sinful lifestyles. I can remember when one of the main campaign issues in the presidential election of 1952 was the fact that Adlai Stevenson was a divorced man. If anyone were to raise that issue today about some political candidate, they would be laughed out of the room.

Another form of blasphemy that has become widespread in America is the use of God's name as a curse word. Shortly after I was born, the movie, "Gone With The Wind," was delayed in its release because it contained the word, "damn." Today, the blatant use of profanity, including taking God's name in vain, is one of the characteristics of American movies. And it is rapidly becoming just as characteristic of American television programs. The sad and sordid state of American entertainment was best summed up by the late Steve Allen when he observed: "In America today, we have vulgarians entertaining barbarians."

The Litany of Sins Continues

The fifth sin Isaiah identified was perhaps the worst of all: "Woe to those who call evil good, and good evil; who substitute darkness for light and light for darkness" (Isaiah 5:20). I would call this the sin of moral perversion.

This is certainly one of the sins of contemporary America. In the latter part of the 20th Century, we began standing traditional morality on its head, calling evil good, and good evil. Pornography was viewed as sexually liberating. Marriage was written off as "old fashioned." Homosexuality was touted as an "acceptable alternative lifestyle." Gambling was converted from a vice into a civic virtue. And the murder of a baby in its mother's womb was declared to be a matter of "freedom of choice."

The next sin Isaiah chose to highlight is a surprising one when you consider the fact that his writings reveal that he was a great intellectual. The sin was intellectual pride: "Woe to those who are wise in their own eyes, and clever in their own sight" (Isaiah 5:21).

As one who spent 20 years of his life teaching at the university level, I have a personal appreciation of what Isaiah is talking about in this verse. It's amazing what a Ph.D. can do for a person's ego, often convincing them that they are the world's greatest expert on literally any subject. Intellectual pride is deeply rooted in America. We believe we can solve any problem if we can only throw enough education at it. We have become zealous humanists, believing we can overcome all problems through intellectual ingenuity.

Intemperance and Corruption

Intemperance is the next sin that Isaiah lists: "Woe to those who are heroes in drinking wine, and valiant men in mixing strong drink" (Isaiah 5:21).

Like Judah, intemperance is epidemic in America today. The latest statistics [2003] show that 15 million Americans are alcoholics, and another 8 million are alcohol abusers. Additionally, 5 million young people between the ages of 14 and 17 are problem drinkers. With regard to drugs, the American scene can best be summed up with one chilling fact: our nation constitutes 5% of the world's population, yet we consume 55% of all the illegal drugs produced in the world!

The last sin Isaiah mentioned was political corruption: "Woe to those . . . who justify the wicked for a bribe, and take away the rights of the ones who are in the right" (Isaiah 5:22-23).

Need I say anything about America's guilt of this sin that has become so ingrained in our political system at every level? I think it is best summed up by the fact that trust of government no longer exists. We expect to be lied to about everything by the politicians and their professional spin doctors.

Summing Up the Sordid Mess

Isaiah summarizes his list of the sins of Judah by presenting the root cause of all of them: "For they have rejected the law of the Lord of hosts, and despised the word of the Holy One of Israel" (Isaiah 5:24). And that is exactly what has happened in the United States. We have turned our back on God, determined to transform America into a secular society with rigid separation of religion from the life of the nation.

Sadly, the mainline denominational churches have contributed to this secular drift by abandoning their belief in the inerrancy of God's Word. They have substituted modern psychology for the preaching of the Word, and their members have been set adrift in a sea of amorality where each person is a law unto himself. Sin has been replaced by "unwise choices." Repentance has given way to the affirmation of a "positive self-image." Salvation has become a matter of "good karma."

It's all a fulfillment of the apostle Paul's prophecy that in the end times, people will hold to a form of religion, but will deny its power (2 Timothy 3:5). We have a lot of religion in America today, but much of it is just that — religion. There is a lot of ritual, but from the pulpit there is a denial of the power of the blood of Jesus and the sufficiency of the Holy Spirit.

Jeremiah's Inventory of Sins

Approximately 70 years after Isaiah compiled his list of the sins of Judah, the Lord called another prophet named Jeremiah and asked him to do the same thing — to go forth throughout the land and conduct a spiritual inventory.

Jeremiah's report is contained in chapters 5 and 6 of his book. Basically, he reported that little had changed since the days of Isaiah. He compiled a list of the same sins Isaiah had identified. The only new ones he added were sexual immorality and religious corruption. With regard to immorality, he reported that adultery was rampant (Jeremiah 5:7-8). Concerning religious corruption, he wrote in astonishment these words (Jeremiah 5:30-31):

> 30 An appalling and horrible thing
> Has happened in the land:

31 The prophets prophesy falsely,
　　And the priests rule on their own authority;
　　And My people love it so!

Both of these problems — immorality and religious corruption — are rampant in America today. The impact of immorality is reflected in the increase in venereal disease and the collapse of the family. Sixty-five million Americans are currently living with an incurable sexually transmitted disease (STD). An additional 15 million become infected with one or more STDs each year, roughly half of whom contract lifelong infections. Due primarily to sexual immorality, 60% of all children in America will spend some time in a single parent family before reaching the age of 18. With the increasing number of births to unmarried women, combined with a continuing high divorce rate, the proportion of children living with one parent has nearly doubled since 1970 [2003 statistics].

Religious corruption in modern America has reached shocking levels. Big time ministries have collapsed like a house of cards due to sexual immorality and financial mismanagement. Christian television is jammed with hucksters preaching God will give you $1,000 if you will give them $100. The ordination of practicing homosexuals and lesbians is becoming more and more common, and some denominations have actually endorsed same-sex marriage in the name of "inclusionary love."

Jeremiah's Summary

Jeremiah provided three summary statements which strike at the heart of America:

- "They have made their faces harder than rock; they have refused to repent" (Jeremiah 5:3).

- "This people has a stubborn and rebellious heart" (Jeremiah 5:23).

- "They do not even know how to blush" (Jeremiah 6:15).

What better summary could you find of the American scene today? Particularly damning is the fact that we no longer know how to blush because we have become so callous to sin. TV talk shows feature incredible immorality, like "mothers who sleep with their daughter's boyfriends." What's amazing — and very revealing — is that when the producers of these shows advertise for these perverts, hundreds respond, eagerly wanting to share their perversion with 40 million Americans. And if anyone dares to stand up in the audience and say, "I think what you are doing is wrong," the audience will turn on them in a fury, shouting, "Who are you to judge?" After all, in America today, it's "different strokes for different folks."

Warnings from God

The blessings and sins of Judah are not the only parallels with the United States. A third thing both nations share in common is warnings from God.

When Judah drifted from God, the Lord sent prophet after prophet to call the nation to repentance and to warn that, if the people refused to repent, God would deliver the nation to destruction. God also warned through remedial judgments like natural disasters and military invasions. His ultimate warning came when He poured out His wrath upon the northern nation of Israel, allowing the nation to be destroyed and its people to be carried into captivity. He instructed the prophets to use Israel's fate as a warning to Judah.

But it was all to no avail. The people of Judah mocked the prophets and refused to recognize any connection between their sins and the calamities that beset them. Jeremiah reported that they scoffed at him, saying that he was full of wind (Jeremiah 5:13). He accused them of being closed minded: "To whom shall I speak and give warning, that they may hear? Behold, their ears are closed, and they cannot listen" (Jeremiah 6:10). They were also arrogant, crying out repeatedly, "This is the temple of the Lord!" (Jeremiah 7:4). What they meant by that statement is that they refused to believe the prophet's warnings of impending national destruction because they did not believe God would allow anyone to destroy His temple.

The American Attitude

The attitude of many Americans is very similar today, even among those who claim to be Christians. God has sent many prophetic voices to call this nation to repentance — men like Dave Wilkerson and Don Wildmon — but just as in the days of Judah, these men's messages have been greeted with scoffing and ridicule. Dave Wilkerson's books have been banned from many church bookstores because they do not contain a "positive message." Don Wildmon reports that many of the most critical letters he receives are from pastors who are annoyed by his campaign against pornography.

I have personally found that when I preach a message of warning about God's impending judgment on this nation, I am often met with incredulity, and sometimes I am even accused of being unpatriotic. I am convinced that many Americans imagine God sitting on His throne wrapped in an American flag. Their attitude is, "God will never touch America because we are a Christian nation, and God needs us to spread the Gospel all over the world."

The first problem with this attitude is that we are not a Christian nation. We are very much a post-Christian nation. In fact, I consider it a blasphemy to refer to the United States as a Christian nation. Like all the nations of the world, we are in rebellion against God. The blood of 50 million aborted babies cries out to God for vengeance. And we serve as the moral polluter of planet earth through the exportation of our sleazy television programs, our filthy movies, our satanic music, and our degrading pornography.

It is also very arrogant to think that God is dependent upon us for anything. He was spreading the Gospel all over the world long before the United States was founded, and He will continue to do so very effectively in the future, even if we disappear from the scene.

In addition to the voices of the prophets, God has been calling this nation to repentance through remedial judgments like the Vietnam War, the AIDS epidemic, and natural disasters like Hurricane Andrew.

God is gracious. Even when He is being taunted to pour out His wrath, He never does so without warning, for He does not wish that any should perish (2 Peter 3:9).

Destruction

Judah refused to repent, and God finally responded by sending the Babylonians to destroy the nation. One of the saddest passages in the Bible is found in 2 Chronicles 36:15-16 where the writer describes God's painful decision to destroy His beloved nation of Judah. It reads as follows:

15 And the Lord, the God of their fathers, sent word to them again and again by His messengers, because He had compassion on His people and on His dwelling place;

16 but they continually mocked the messengers of God, despised His words and scoffed at His prophets, until the wrath of the Lord arose against His people, until there was no remedy.

Judah was destroyed for committing the same sins that characterize the United States today. Why should our fate be any different?

● We have been blessed like Judah.

● We have sinned like Judah.

- We are now being warned like Judah.

- We are responding like Judah.

- The conclusion seems inescapable: We are heading for the same fate as Judah.

What is that fate likely to be? What form will it take? And is there any hope that we might avoid the fate of Judah?

For the answers to these questions, let's take a look at the meaning of the attack on America that occurred on September 11, 2001.

The Battle Hymn of the Republic
(Fifth Verse)

In the beauty of the lilies
    Christ was born across the sea,
With a glory in His bosom
    that transfigures you and me;
As He died to make men holy,
    let us die to make men free
While God is marching on.

Glory! Glory! Hallelujah!
Glory! Glory! Hallelujah!
Glory! Glory! Hallelujah!
His truth is marching on.

When the Civil War broke out, there was no great national anthem that was generally accepted as such. During 1861 a national contest was conducted to produce a new patriotic song. A total of 1,200 entries were received, and none were considered worthy.

In December of 1861 Julia Ward Stowe (1819-1910), an unknown poet, visited the Army of the Potomac where she heard the soldiers singing one of their favorite marching songs, "John Brown's Body." She decided they needed some more appropriate words for the song. When she returned to her home in Boston, she showed her new words to the editor of the *Atlantic Monthly*. He suggested the title, and published her poem in the issue of February 1862. The song became an instant sensation.

Chapter 4

The Meaning of 9/11:
Did we get the message?

"Righteousness exalts a nation,
But sin is a disgrace to any people."
Proverbs 14:34

Two questions began to pour into our office via email and telephone on the day that the horrific attack on America occurred. Why did the attack happen — what motivated it? And why would God allow such incredible carnage?

I believe there are three keys to understanding why the attack occurred:

1. It related to America's support of Israel.

2. It related to the inherent nature of Islam.

3. It related to America's rebellion against God.

Support of Israel

The most obvious answer to why America would be attacked by Islamic terrorists is our support of the nation of Israel, and that certainly is an important factor. Muslims hate the Jews with a passion, and their loudly proclaimed goal is to exterminate the nation of Israel, or, as they have so often put it, "to make the Mediterranean run red with the blood of the Jews."

The Muslims feel obligated to seek this goal of annihilation because of the teachings of their holy book, the Koran. Their scriptures tell them that they have a responsibility to conquer the world for their god, Allah. And they are further taught that this responsibility is particularly urgent with regard to any territory that has been won for Allah and subsequently lost. That principle applies to Israel, which for many years was controlled by Muslims as the land of Palestine.

Since the United States has been the only nation willing to stand behind Israel, the Muslims believe that if they can make that commitment painful enough for us, we will abandon Israel. They may be right. I have already heard many people on call-in shows on the radio state that we need "to cut Israel loose" so that the terrorists will stop targeting us.

The Nature of Islam

But this idea ignores a deeper source of the hatred that the Muslims have toward the United States. The fact of the matter is that if Israel were to disappear from the world scene tomorrow, the Muslim world would still hate America with a passion.

That's because Islam is a cultural religion whose purpose is to impose by force, if necessary, a Seventh Century Arabic culture on the entire world. The truth is that Islam is a virulent form of cultural imperialism. This is very difficult for Westerners to comprehend. For example, Christianity is "supra-cultural" in the sense that it allows people to live, dress, and eat in accordance with the culture in which they exist. Not so with Islam. Islam regulates every aspect of life to the point that culture, religion, and politics are inseparable. There is no separation of the mosque and state in Islamic nations.

There is not one Islamic nation where democracy exists. Freedom of religion is non-existent in the Islamic world. No Islamic state will allow the open proclamation of the Gospel. Jews are anathema.

Islam by its very nature is incompatible with modern life and democracy. The United States is viewed as the "Great Satan" because we lead the world in technology and we are the major advocate of democratic principles. We are considered to be the most important threat to the purity of Islam.

We are also hated because of our power. Islam has always been a religion of the sword. The very word, Islam, means "submission." Every place where Islam prevails, the religion has been imposed by military conquest. It is still the goal of Islam to conquer the world, and the United States is viewed as the major obstacle to that goal.

Do not be deceived by all the media talk about Islamic fundamentalists being unrepresentative of true Islam. The Koran not only condones violence against unbelievers, it actually commands it: "Fight and slay the pagans wherever you find them, and seize them, beleaguer them, and lie in wait for them in every stratagem of war" (Sura 9:5). As for those who resist conversion to Islam, the Koran issues the following command: "Their punishment is . . . execution, or crucifixion, or the cutting off of hands and feet from the opposite sides, or exile from the land" (Sura 5:33).

Do not be deceived by all the assertions of liberal, apostate Christian leaders who claim that the Islamic peoples are our "brothers and sisters in the Lord" because they worship the same God that Christians do. Allah is not the God of the Bible. Allah is an unknowable, aloof, impersonal, and capricious god who saves or condemns people on the basis of their works. The Koran states that Jews are people "whom Allah has cursed" (Sura 4:52). The Trinity is specifically denied (Sura 5:73-75) and Jesus is dismissed as nothing more than "an apostle of Allah" (Sura 4:171).

In short, Islam is a demonic religion that is the very antithesis of Christianity.

America's Rebellion

The third reason the attacks occurred relates to what has been happening inside America since the 1960's. As I have often said, and as I tried to document in a previous book,

Living for Christ in the End Times, the United States is a nation in rebellion against God.

This fact was summed up in a powerful way in a poem by Judge Roy Moore, the former Chief Justice of the Supreme Court of Alabama. He is the judge who refused to remove the Ten Commandments from his court room despite demands and lawsuits by the ACLU. Here is a portion of his poem, entitled "America the Beautiful?"

> America the Beautiful,
> Or so you used to be.
> Land of the pilgrim's pride,
> I'm glad they'll never see
> Babies piled in dumpsters,
> Abortion on demand,
> Oh, sweet land of liberty,
> Your house is built on sand.
>
> Our children wander aimlessly,
> Poisoned by cocaine,
> Choosing to indulge their lusts,
> When God has said abstain.
> From sea to shining sea,
> Our nation turns away
> From the teaching of God's love
> And a need to always pray.
>
> So many worldly pastors
> Tell lies about our Rock,
> Saying God is going broke
> So they can fleece the flock.
> We've kept God in our temples,
> How callous we have grown,
> When earth is but His footstool
> And Heaven is His throne.
>
> You think that God's not angry
> That our land's a moral slum?

> How much longer will He wait
> Before His judgment comes?
> How are we to face our God
> From whom we cannot hide?
> What then is left for us to do,
> But stem this evil tide?

We are in the process of jettisoning our Christian heritage. Christian leaders are denying the fundamentals of the faith. Political leaders are determined to convert us into a secular society. Americans have responded by embracing a hedonistic lifestyle. In the words of Judge Robert H. Bork, ever since the mid-20th Century, we have been "slouching towards Gomorrah." In the process, as I said before, we have become the moral polluter of planet earth through the exportation of our immoral and violent television programs and movies.

A Startling Response to Prayer

A graphic illustration of how far this nation has drifted from its Christian roots can be found in the response to a prayer that was presented before the Kansas State House of Representatives in January of 1996. The prayer was delivered by Joe Wright, pastor of Central Christian Church in Wichita.

The prayer prompted several legislators to walk out. Others called a press conference and denounced it. The Democrat House Minority Leader said it "reflects the extreme, radical views that continue to dominate the House Republican agenda since right-wing extremists seized control of the House Republican caucus last year."

What was said in this prayer that caused such an uproar? Well, read it for yourself:

> Heavenly Father, we come before You to ask Your
> forgiveness and to seek Your direction and guidance.
> We know Your Word says, "Woe to those who call
> evil good," but that is exactly what we have done.
> We have lost our spiritual equilibrium and reversed

our values.

We have ridiculed the absolute truth of Your Word in the name of moral pluralism.

We have worshiped other gods and called it multiculturalism.

We have endorsed perversion and called it an alternative lifestyle.

We have exploited the poor and called it a lottery.

We have neglected the needy and called it self-preservation.

We have rewarded laziness and called it welfare.

We have killed our unborn and called it choice.

We have shot abortionists and called it justifiable.

We have neglected to discipline our children and called it building self-esteem.

We have abused power and called it political savvy.

We have coveted our neighbor's possessions and called it ambition.

We have polluted the air with profanity and pornography and called it freedom of expression.

We have ridiculed the time-honored values of our forefathers and called it enlightenment.

Search us, O God, and know our hearts today. Try us and see if there be some wicked way in us. Cleanse us from every sin and set us free.

Guide and bless these men and women who have been sent here by the people of Kansas and who have been ordained by You to govern this great state.

Grant them Your wisdom to rule, and may their decisions direct us to the center of Your will. And, as we continue our prayer and as we come in out of the fog, give us clear minds to accomplish our goals as we begin this Legislature. For we pray in Jesus' name, Amen.

As you can see, the prayer was a powerful expression of our nation's Christian heritage, expressing the fundamental values that have made our nation great. Yet, some of the politicians responded in rage because the prayer was not "politically correct."

The Relation to 9/11

How does all this relate to why the attacks of September 11 took place? I would assert that the attacks were permitted by God as a judgment on the United States for the sins of our nation, for our rebellion against God and His Word.

I therefore see the attacks as a spiritual wake-up call from the Lord. Think about it for a moment — God allowed the symbols of American pride to be attacked, the symbols of both wealth and power: the Trade Towers in New York and the Pentagon in Washington, D.C.

We must face up to the unpleasant reality that we are a nation in rebellion against God. And we must realize that our rebellion is particularly dangerous. The reason is that we have been blessed more abundantly with freedom, prosperity, and spiritual riches than any other nation in history. Why is this so significant? Because the Word of God teaches that those to whom much is given, much is expected (Luke 12:47-48). That means we are going to be held to a higher level of accountability than other nations. And it means our rebellion is going to be judged more harshly.

As we began turning our back on God during the 20th Century, God started placing judgments upon us to call us to repentance. The Vietnam War was a judgment. Additional judgments included the drug epidemic, the homosexual scourge, the AIDS plague, the glut of pornography, and the rebellion of young people.

The first chapter of Romans teaches that God pours out His wrath on a rebellious nation by stepping back, lowering His hedge of protection, and allowing evil to multiply. It's as if He were saying, "If you really want to live in a fouled nest, then I will let you." According to Romans 1, when He first steps back, a sexual revolution occurs (Romans 1:24-25). That happened in the United States in the 1960's. If the society persists in its rebellion, then God will take another step back and lower His hedge of protection even more. The result will be a plague of homosexuality (Romans 1:26-27). The United States has been experiencing this judgment since the 1970's. If the society continues its rebellion, God will take a third step back and deliver the nation to a "depraved mind" (Romans 1:28-31). This is the point at which the Lord moves the nation from judgment to destruction. We are at that point.

We have dug in our heels and set our jaw against God. We are shaking our fist at Him, saying, "Who are You to try to tell us what to do?" We are thumbing our nose at the very One who has blessed us beyond anything we have ever deserved.

So, I believe that God allowed the attacks of September 11, 2001 in order to get our attention — to call our nation to repentance before He is forced by His character to deliver us from judgment to destruction.

God's Sovereignty

Now, I know that many Christians have great difficulty with the idea that God could allow such horror to take place. We want to just flippantly write it all off as "the work of Satan."

The interesting thing is that the Bible has no such difficulty. In the Bible, all calamities are ascribed to God, whether they be natural disasters or acts of war. That's because God is sovereign. He is in control. Nothing can happen without His permission. That's why when Satan wanted to touch Job, he first had to ask God's permission (Job 1:6-12).

Keep in mind that God has a perfect will and a permissive will. For example, the Bible states point blank that God does not wish that any should perish, but that all should come to repentance (2 Peter 3:9). In other words, it is God's perfect will that all people be saved. But in His permissive will, God allows people to use their free will to reject Him and thus be lost.

God has a perfect will for history. It will result in the triumph of Jesus as King of kings and Lord of lords, ruling over all the nations of the world, with the world flooded with peace, righteousness, and justice. As God moves toward the accomplishment of that goal, He must deal with the evil of Satan and Man.

Thankfully, ***God has the wisdom and power to orchestrate all the evil of both Satan and Man to the triumph of Jesus.***

The Example of Habakkuk

The Bible is full of examples of this fundamental truth. One that comes to mind is found in the book of Habakkuk. The prophet was one of many God called to preach a message of repentance to Judah, warning the people that if they did not repent, they would suffer God's wrath.

Habakkuk did as the Lord directed, and his message was despised. He was ridiculed and rebuked. Finally, Habakkuk cried out to God, asking Him to validate the prophet's message by sending judgments upon the nation. The Lord astounded him by revealing that He was about to send the Chaldeans to completely destroy Judah.

Habakkuk wanted some wrath from God to fall on his nation, but he wanted just a little. The idea that God was about to send the most evil nation in the world to destroy Judah was beyond his comprehension. He responded by asking the Lord a very profound question: "How can You who are holy, just and righteous punish those who are evil with those who are more evil?" The Lord responded by saying, "The righteous shall live by faith."

It was a tough answer. The Lord was in effect saying, "Who are you to question Me? Your duty is to trust Me, not to question Me."

As Habakkuk wrestled with this difficult answer, the Lord helped him by giving him a very dramatic vision of the Second Coming of the Messiah, showing Habakkuk that when that event occurs, the Messiah will pour out the wrath of God on all the nations of the world (Habakkuk 3:3-15). Reassured with God's eternal perspective, Habakkuk responded by singing a great song of tough faith in which he asserted that even if the Lord sent the army and destroyed his nation, he would "exult in the Lord [and] . . . rejoice in the God of my salvation [for] the Lord God is my strength" (Habakkuk 3:18-19).

Well, God did send the army. The city of Jerusalem was destroyed. The sacred Temple was burned. The nation of Judah was destroyed. The Jewish people were taken into exile. But today, 2,500 years later, the Jewish people have been regathered from the four corners of the earth and re-established in their land. The Chaldeans are in the dustbin of history. God used an evil nation, the Chaldeans, to discipline the Jews, and then He raised up the Medo-Persian Empire to demolish the Chaldeans.

Bringing Good Out of War

History is also full of examples of God working through the evil schemes of Satan and Man to accomplish His purposes. Take World War I as an example. Satan must have thought he had accomplished one of his greatest successes when he maneuvered the armies of the world into the mass slaughter that took place at the beginning of the 20th Century on the battlefields of Europe. Yet God worked through that evil to implement His end time program for the return of His Son.

The point is that World War I resulted in the liberation of the land of Palestine from 400 years of Turkish rule. The land was handed over to the British as a League of Nations Mandate, and the British immediately announced that their intention was to turn it into a homeland for the Jewish people.

This must have panicked Satan because he knows Bible prophecy, and he therefore knows that the Bible says the Messiah will return when the Jews have been regathered to their land and are once again in control of Jerusalem (Zechariah 12). So, Satan responded by orchestrating World War II and the Nazi Holocaust. His intention was to annihilate the Jews so that God could not fulfill His promise to regather them. But God preserved the Jews through the war, and in the process He motivated them to return to their homeland. They came out of the Holocaust saying, "Never again! Never again will we submit ourselves to a Hitler. We will have our own land and our own state."

God worked through the evil of World War I to prepare the land for the people. In like manner, He worked through the evil of World War II to prepare the people for the land.

Satan has to be the most frustrated character on planet earth. No matter what he throws at God, the Lord takes it and turns it around for good.

God and Evil

Now, let me make one thing very clear: ***God is not the source of evil***. Evil originates from the free will of Satan and Man when they use that free will to rebel against God.

But God allows evil to succeed at times for a multiplicity of reasons, some known only to Him. The reasons that we can discern include the following: to test us, to discipline us, and to sanctify us. Sometimes God allows evil to come into our lives to test us — not to determine how strong we are (He already knows), but to show us how weak we are so that we will lean on Him. At other times, God allows us to suffer because He desires to discipline us for drifting out of His will. The Bible says God disciplines those whom He loves (Hebrews 12:5-6). Suffering is also essential to sanctification — to being shaped more fully into the image of Jesus. For example, how could you ever show compassion toward a sick person if you have never been ill?

Bringing Good Out of Evil

To demonstrate again how God can work through evil acts to accomplish good, consider the tragedy of Pearl Harbor. Before that attack, public opinion polls in the United States showed that 75 to 80 percent of Americans opposed American entry into the war in Europe. Americans were overwhelmingly isolationist. Pearl Harbor changed all that in a matter of minutes. It catapulted us into the war and sealed the fate of the Nazis. A terrible tragedy worked for good.

I believe our second Pearl Harbor of September 11, 2001, was a call for national repentance. It was a call for us to get on our knees and repent of our sins — to repent of our material-ism, our hedonism, our idolatry, our pride, and our slaughter of more than 50 million babies since 1973.

God loves us. He has richly blessed us. He has worked through us to spread the Gospel all over the world. He does not want to deliver us from judgment to destruction. But He will do so, just as He has done with other rebellious nations, if we do not repent. In fact, He *must* do so because His justice, righteousness, and holiness demand it.

Reluctant Conclusions

I personally believe we will not repent and that we will therefore experience the wrath of God. I believe this is the reason the United States is not mentioned in end time Bible prophecy.

If we continue on our present course of rebellion against God, I believe the Lord will have no choice but to humble us by pouring out a decisive judgment upon us. We will suddenly cease to be a world power, and we will therefore play no significant role in end time events.

How could this be? There are several possible scenarios.

Economic Collapse

The first thing that comes to mind is an economic catastrophe that will result from our out of control debt situation. The official outstanding debt of the U.S. government is currently 6.2 trillion dollars [2003]. That amounts to $21,540 per person. This debt is increasing at the rate of 1.1 billion per day! Private debt is even more horrendous. At the beginning of the 21st Century, there was a staggering $25.6 trillion of credit market debt outstanding in the U.S. That total represents a doubling of the debt burden since 1990. America's total debt, public and private (including state and local government) stands at around $32 trillion dollars! That's $115,322 per man, woman, and child. Amazingly, 52% of this debt was accumulated in the 1990s, a decade driven primarily by debt instead of productivity [all statistics are 2003].

There is no way to escape the conclusion that America has become a debt junkie. We are living on money we do not have and will never have, and sooner or later the weight of this debt is going to collapse our economy. One irony is that we have killed 50 million babies who could have been in the work force today contributing to our economic health by producing goods and services and paying taxes.

I believe an unprecedented economic collapse is highly likely because money is the real god of America, and the true God of this universe is a jealous One who does not tolerate idolatry. God, by His very nature, is going to be compelled to destroy our false god.

External Attack

Another possible fate for the United States is destruction from a Russian nuclear attack. This, of course, could happen in conjunction with an economic collapse, or it could be the cause of that collapse.

The reason a Russian attack is so likely is because the Bible says that the Russians will lead an end time invasion of Israel (Ezekiel 38 and 39). Since we are Israel's only ally, it seems inconceivable to me that the Russians would attack Israel without unleashing a pre-emptive nuclear attack on us in order to prevent us from coming to Israel's defense.

This attack may be hinted at in Ezekiel 39:6 where it says that at the time of the Russian invasion, fire will fall on "those who inhabit the coastlands in safety." The Russian attack would come most probably from submarines deployed off our East and West coasts. Each Russian submarine carries more fire power than all the bombs dropped in World War II. Such an attack would give us only seven minutes, not even enough time to launch a counter attack.

Some argue that since the collapse of the Soviet government, Russia is now too weak to launch any attack against Israel or the United States. It is true that the economy of Russia is in shambles [2003], but the military power is intact, including thousands of nuclear warheads. The truth of the matter is that Russia is far more dangerous today than before the Soviet collapse. The increased danger is due to the instability of the government and the chaos in the economy.

There is no hope for democracy in Russia because the societal values that are essential for the working of a democratic system do no exist. Nor is there any historical experience with democracy. Before the Commissars were the Czars.

The current experiment with a quasi-democratic system will not last long. It will be overthrown, most likely by a coup that will produce a military dictatorship. That new tyranny will then most likely resort to one of the oldest techniques of government — namely, stirring up trouble abroad to divert people's attention away from their domestic problems.

Internal Attack

Another way in which American power could be rapidly dissipated is through internal terrorist attacks. Just stop and think for a moment about the overwhelming impact that the 9/11 attack had upon our society and economy. In the months that followed, the stock markets lost over 7 trillion dollars in value. The travel industry (airlines and hotels) was devastated. Civil liberties were severely curtailed. And don't forget that our national government was brought to a standstill by the subsequent anthrax scare.

Multiply such terrorist attacks, including the poisoning of water supplies and the explosion of "dirty bombs" containing nuclear waste materials, and you can readily see how our nation could be brought to its knees. In fact, it is not beyond the realm of possibility that terrorists could detonate an atomic bomb that has been smuggled into one of our major ports aboard a cargo ship. No matter how vigilant we may be, in the final analysis, there is no way to protect against terrorists who have no regard for their own lives, much less those who believe that dying for their cause will guarantee their entry into paradise.

Internal Rot

Internal collapse could also result from the moral rot that has our nation by its throat. This is what ultimately destroyed the Roman Empire, and it is what led to the sudden collapse of Soviet Russia.

As we have abandoned our Judeo-Christian heritage, we have evolved into an amoral society that has lost its respect for the sanctity of life. Individualism has been carried to the brink of anarchy as everyone does what is right in his own eyes. Greed is fracturing our society between young and old, rich and poor, black and white. Class warfare could easily deteriorate into civil warfare with outbreaks of uncontrollable violence in our major cities.

The collapse of Soviet Russia is a good example of how suddenly a great empire can fall. Despite the fact that it had the world's strongest military power, the whole corrupt Communist system fell apart literally overnight. The economy went with it, and people were quickly reduced to bartering for food and clothing.

I saw it all first hand. The suddenness and severity of it would have been hard to believe otherwise. As I walked the streets of Moscow in 1992 observing the suffering of the people, the Lord impressed a message on my heart:

> Go back home and hold up Soviet Russia as an example to the American people. Use it to show them how quickly I can bring an empire to its knees. Call for America to repent before it is too late.

It was the same kind of message God had laid on the hearts of the prophets of Judah when the Assyrians destroyed their sister nation of Israel.

Another Alternative

There is another scenario that could explain the silence about America in the Scriptures. It is the fact that the United States would be suddenly destroyed by the Rapture of the Church.

There is no doubt that the Rapture would devastate contemporary America. We have more born again Christians than any other nation in the world — more than all of Western Europe and England combined. Only 7% of the British attend church anymore, and many of those are going to churches that are completely apostate. Less than 3% of the people of Western Europe are evangelical Christians. In contrast, 23% of Americans are evangelicals, a total of 65 million.

Another factor that would make the Rapture so devastating to the United States is that we have many evangelical Christians in high positions of leadership, in both government and business. The sudden removal of these people would throw our whole society into chaos.

Christian Culpability

If America must be destroyed, as I think it must be, then I would certainly prefer that it be the result of the Rapture.

Perhaps it will be. I hope that is the case.

But I doubt it. It is likely to be only the *coup de grâce*. God must deal with sin, and much of the sin of our nation is due to Christians who are either participating in it or else refusing to speak out against it. I have often said that if Christians would stop getting abortions, the slaughter houses would have to close. If Christians would stop gambling, the lotteries would have to shut down. If Christians would stop going to R rated movies, Hollywood would have to stop making them. I could go on and on with many other examples, but the point is clear: Christians are a part of the problem.

That also applies to taking a stand for righteousness. Just as hundreds of thousands of Christians looked the other way and sat silently while six million Jews were murdered in Germany, millions of Christians in America are unwilling to stand up and be counted for righteousness.

The Bible never promises that the saved will be immune to suffering and calamity. In fact, it teaches that the rain falls on the just and the unjust. What God's Word does promise is that the Lord will walk through the suffering with us, ministering to us and providing our basic needs. Here's how the promise is put in Isaiah 43:1-2 —

> 1 Do not fear, for I have redeemed you;
> I have called you by name, you are Mine!

> 2 When you pass through the waters,
> I will be with you;
> And through the rivers, they will not overflow you.
> When you walk through the fire,
> you will not be scorched.
> Nor will the flame burn you.

The prophet Nahum expressed the same concept in these words: "The Lord is good, a stronghold in the day of trouble, and He knows those who take refuge in Him" (Nahum 1:7). King David expressed it this way: "Even though I walk through the valley of the shadow of death, I fear no evil, for You are with me" (Psalm 23:4).

Our Ultimate National Destiny

Regardless of how we are removed from the international scene as a world power, we are most likely to end up absorbed into the European Union as one of its members states. This seems only natural in view of all the historic and cultural ties we have with that part of the world.

The Bible indicates that during the Tribulation the world will be divided into four power blocs. "The king of the North" (Daniel 11:40) will most likely be a coalition of nations led by Russia. "The king of the South" (Daniel 11:40) appears to be the leader of Egypt who will probably head up a bloc of Muslim nations. "The kings of the East" (Revelation 16:12) consist of an alliance of Asian leaders who rebel against the Antichrist and march to Armageddon to make war with him (Daniel 11:40-45). The king of the West will, of course, be the Antichrist and his European confederation, which most likely will include the Western Hemisphere and the United States after its downfall.

So, where does this leave us? Is there any hope for the United States at all? Is our fate sealed? Are we doomed?

Before we consider these important questions, let's pause for a look at another significant remedial judgment our nation has experienced — namely, Hurricane Katrina.

America the Beautiful?

The United States in Bible Prophecy

2006

My Country 'Tis of Thee
(also known as "America")

My country 'tis of thee,
Sweet land of liberty,
Of thee I sing.
Land where my fathers died!
Land of the Pilgrim's pride!
From every mountain side,
Let freedom ring!

Our father's God, to Thee,
Author of liberty,
To Thee we sing.
Long may our land be bright,
With freedom's holy light;
Protect us by Thy might,
Great God, our King!

The author of this great patriotic song was Samuel Francis Smith (1808-1895). He attended Harvard University and Andover Theological Seminary before entering the ministry as an ordained Baptist preacher in 1832.

That same year he was looking through a German hymnal when he discovered a catchy tune.

I instantly felt the impulse to write a patriotic hymn of my own, adapted to the tune. Picking up a scrap of waste paper which lay near me, I wrote at once, probably within half an hour, the hymn "Amer ica" as it is now known everywhere.

The tune is the same one that is used for the national anthem of England.

Chapter 5

The Message of Katrina:
Was it the handwriting on the wall?

There will be great earthquakes, and in various places plagues and famines; and there will be terrors and great signs from heaven. — Luke 21:11

There are many spiritual lessons to be learned from the Hurricane Katrina tragedy. One of the most important is the way the storm showed the importance of life over things. Life is precious. Things — all the material items we collect and become so attached to — are disposable. The storm also drove home the fact that life can be very tenuous, and we therefore need to live with an eternal perspective.

But I believe the most important message of the storm was prophetic in nature, and I believe that message relates to the fate of America.

The Signs of the Times

The Bible provides us with many signs we are to watch for that will signal the soon return of Jesus. As I have studied them, I have found it useful to put them into categories. They naturally seem to fall into six groups:

1) The Signs of Nature

2) The Signs of Society

3) Spiritual Signs

4) The Signs of World Politics

5) The Signs of Technology

6) The Signs of Israel

The Signs in Summary

God has always spoken through signs of nature. We will consider these in detail later.

The signs of society relate to the fact that Jesus said that right before His return society will become "like the days of Noah" (Matthew 24:37). If you go to Genesis 6 and read about that society, you will find that it was characterized by immorality and violence. The Apostle Paul reiterated the prophecy in 2 Timothy 3 where he said that society in the end times will fall apart as men become lovers of self, lovers of money, and lovers of pleasure.

The spiritual signs are numerous and fall into two categories — negative and positive. The negative ones are extremely negative in nature. They include the rise of false christs and false prophets, the spread of heresy and apostasy, the persecution of believers, and an epidemic of spiritual deception. But, thank God, there are also positive spiritual signs we are to watch for, the most important being a great outpouring of the Holy Spirit as manifested by the spread of the gospel all over the world.

The signs of world politics relate to the fact that the Bible presents a certain configuration of nations in the end times. The prophecies include the re-establishment of Israel, the attacks of the Arabs against Israel, the menace of Russia to Israel, and the rebirth of the Roman Empire from which the Antichrist will arise.

When I refer to "signs of technology," I have in mind end time prophecies that can only be understood in the light of modern technological developments. It's interesting that even the biblical prophets did not always understand their prophecies. In Daniel 12, when the prophet complained about the problem, the Lord responded by saying that the prophecies would not be understood until the end times (Daniel 12:9). The fact that we are understanding prophecies today that have never been understood before is proof positive that we are in the end times.

Let me give you an example of what I am talking about. Revelation 11 says that two great witnesses of God will prophesy in Jerusalem during the first half of the Tribulation, serving as the conscience of the world. We are then told that they will be killed by the Antichrist, and their bodies will lie in the streets of Jerusalem for three and a half days *while all the world looks upon them.* This prophecy was not understandable until after the first satellite was launched in 1957. Today, we think nothing of the prophecy because we know that all you have to do to enable the whole world to look upon the bodies is to point a TV camera at them and then zap the signal up to a satellite.

The Most Significant Signs

The signs of Israel are the most important, more important than all the rest put together. The reason is that the Jews are God's prophetic time clock. This means that God often points to future events and says they will occur when certain things happen to the Jews. A good example can be found in Luke 21:24 where Jesus is quoted as saying that He would return "when Jerusalem is no longer trampled down by the Gentiles."

There are four major prophecies concerning Israel whose fulfillment we are told will identify the end times. They are as follows:

1) The Jews will be regathered to Israel from the four corners of the earth (Isaiah 11:11-12). The fulfillment of this prophecy began in the 1890's and continues to this day.

2) The state of Israel will be re-established (Isaiah 66:7-8 and Ezekiel 37:11-12). This prophecy was fulfilled on May 14, 1948.

3) The Jews will re-occupy the city of Jerusalem (Zechariah 8:4-8). This prophecy was fulfilled on June 7, 1967.

4) The whole world will come against Israel over the issue of who will control Jerusalem (Zechariah 12:1-3). The fulfillment of this prophecy began in 1991 when the United States joined the rest of the world's nations in applying pressure to force Israel to surrender at least half of Jerusalem.

As you can see from the fulfillment of the four signs above, we are clearly on the threshold of the Tribulation, and that means we are living on borrowed time.

A Category Held in Contempt

The category of signs that receives the least respect is the signs of nature. There are two reasons for this, one that is conceptual, and another that is philosophical.

The conceptual problem resides in the fact that there have always been signs of nature. So, when confronted with the prophesied signs of nature, many people shrug their shoulders and ask, "What else is new? There have always been tornados, hurricanes, and earthquakes."

What they overlook is that Jesus said these signs would be like "birth pangs" (Matthew 24:8). That means they will increase in frequency and intensity the closer we get to the Lord's return. And that is exactly what appears to be happening today.

The philosophical problem many people have with the signs of nature is due to the fact that we have been brainwashed by Western scientific rationalism into believing that for something to exist, you must be able to see it, measure it, weigh it, and dissect it. In contrast, the Bible teaches there is a whole realm of the supernatural that cannot normally be perceived by the senses. This realm includes angels, demons, and the operation of the Holy Spirit. It also includes God's intervention from time to time through natural disasters.

God and Signs of Nature

Sometimes God uses signs of nature to underline the importance of major events. Thus, at the birth of Jesus, God placed a special light in the heavens, probably a manifestation of His Shekinah glory. When Jesus was crucified, the earth experienced three hours of darkness and a major earthquake. And the Bible says that when Jesus returns, the world will experience the greatest earthquake in its history. Every island will be moved, valleys will be lifted, mountains will be lowered, and the city of Jerusalem will be lifted up like a jewel, possibly becoming the highest place on earth (Revelation 16:18-21 and Isaiah 40:3-5).

More often, God uses signs of nature as remedial judgments to call nations to repentance. Both the Bible and history attest to the fact that God has a pattern of dealing with nations. To begin with, as I demonstrated in chapter 1, He is the one who establishes nations, and He is the one who takes them down (Daniel 2:20-21). When a nation rebels against God, He responds first by raising up prophetic voices to call the nation to repentance. These are not people with supernatural knowledge of the future. They simply have the gift of discernment to see where a nation is missing God's mark. To put it another way, they know how to apply the Scriptures to contemporary events.

If a nation refuses to listen to the prophetic voices, God will then send remedial judgments. These can take many forms. Deuteronomy 28 mentions economic failure, rebellion of youth, an epidemic of divorce, confusion in government, foreign domination, and military defeat. The chapter also mentions natural disasters like drought, crop failure, and pestilence.

Finally, if a nation digs in against God and sets its jaw against His calls to repentance, a point of no return will be reached — often referred to as "when the wound becomes incurable" (Nahum 3:19, Jeremiah 30:12, and Micah 1:9). At this point, the Lord will deliver the nation from judgment to destruction. That destruction may occur quickly — as with Babylon and the Soviet Union — or it may occur gradually over a period of time, as with the Roman Empire.

Examples of Remedial Judgments

There are many examples of remedial judgments in the Bible that involve natural disasters. Take for example the plagues with which God afflicted Egypt in order to convince Pharaoh that he should release the children of Israel from captivity (Exodus 7-11). The Lord sent plagues of frogs, gnats, flies, and locusts. In addition, He contaminated the nation's water, afflicted the livestock with pestilence, struck the people with sores and boils, engulfed the land in a thick darkness, and finally took the lives of the first born of both men and live-stock.

When King Ahab led the Israelites into the worship of a pagan god, the Lord raised up the prophet Elijah to call the king and his people to repentance. When they ignored Elijah, the Lord then put a remedial judgment on the land in the form of a severe three and a half year drought (1 Kings 17 and 18).

The book of Joel tells about a locust invasion that afflicted Judah. This was one of the worst calamities that could befall an agricultural society. It appears that people began bemoaning their "bad luck," when God sent the prophet Joel to inform them that the disaster had nothing to do with luck. Joel boldly proclaimed that the locusts had been sent by God to call the people to repentance. He warned that if they did not repent, the Lord would send something even worse — an enemy army. The people ignored Joel and the prophets who followed him, and God ultimately sent the army, delivering them from judgment to destruction.

Seventy years later when the Babylonian captivity ended, the Jews who returned to Judah laid the foundation for a new temple and then quickly lost interest in the project. They turned their attention instead to the building of their personal homes. For 14 years the foundation of the temple stood vacant. Finally, God raised up an elderly, tough-talking prophet named Haggai. He confronted the people by asking them: "Have you noticed that when you plant your crops, they are destroyed by root rot? And when you replant them, they are destroyed again by hail? And when you replant, a wind storm comes? God is speaking to you! He is calling you to repent of your misplaced priorities and give attention to the rebuilding of His temple." For once, the people listened, obeyed, and were blessed (Haggai 1).

The Nature of God

God has continued throughout history to use signs of nature to call nations to repentance. Some people say, "Oh no, God doesn't do that anymore because this is the 'Age of Grace.'"

The first problem with that statement is that it implies there was a previous time of no grace. The fact of the matter is that there is only one way of salvation that has ever existed: namely, grace through faith (Joel 2:32).

Furthermore, the Bible says God is "the same yesterday, today and forever" (Hebrews 13:8). There is no such thing as the Old Testament God of wrath and the New Testament God of grace. God does not change (Malachi 3:6).

The so-called Old Testament God of wrath is the one who showed grace toward the wicked city of Ninevah when its people repented in response to the message of Jonah. The so-called New Testament God of grace is the one who warned the church at Thyatira that if it continued to tolerate a false prophetess, He would "cast her upon a bed of sickness and those who commit adultery with her into great tribulation." Further, He threatened to "kill her children with pestilence" (Revelation 2:22-23).

Our God is a God of grace, mercy, and love. But He is also a God of holiness, righteousness, and justice. The balanced view of God is presented by the prophet Nahum. Speaking of God's grace, he wrote: "The Lord is good, a stronghold in the day of trouble, and He knows those who take refuge in Him" (Nahum 1:7).

But Nahum warned that the same God is one who is righteous and holy and who will not tolerate sin (Nahum 1:2-3):

> A jealous and avenging God is the Lord;
> The Lord is avenging and wrathful.
> The Lord takes vengeance on His adversaries,
> And He reserves wrath for His enemies.
> The Lord is slow to anger and great in power,
> And the Lord will by no means leave the guilty
>   unpunished.

The Role of Satan

Some counter by trying to argue that natural calamities come from Satan and not God. But the Bible teaches that God is sovereign. Satan is not free to do anything he pleases. When he wanted to torment Job, he had to ask God's permission, and when he was granted permission, God laid down rules about what he could and could not do (Job 1:6-12).

The Bible says God does not tempt us (James 1:13). Yet Jesus taught us to pray, "Lead us not into temptation" (Matthew 6:13). How can these statements be reconciled? The answer is that although Satan is the tempter, he cannot do so unless God allows it.

Again, God is sovereign, and nothing happens that He does not allow, either in His perfect will or His permissive will.

That is the reason the Bible attributes all natural disasters to God.

Crucial Questions

Are all natural calamities a product of Man's sin? Yes, absolutely. The original creation was perfect. Natural calamities are a result of the curse that God placed on the creation in response to Man's sin. When Jesus returns, the curse will be lifted and natural calamities will cease.

Do all natural calamities represent remedial judgments of God? No — most are products of the natural processes of our weather systems.

How then can we determine when a natural calamity is a remedial judgment? One important factor is the timing of the event as it relates to the sins of the nation. Another factor is the magnitude of the event. Remedial judgments are designed to have great shock value in order to capture people's attention and force them to think with an eternal perspective. The most important factor is God's Spirit witnessing to the spirits of those to whom He has given the gift of prophecy. They will be motivated to speak forth with a united voice.

The Example of the United States

We can see all these principles operating in the history of our own nation. We were founded as a Christian nation, committed to Christian values, and God greatly blessed us. But in the 1960's we began to thumb our nose at God as a cultural revolution was launched. Our society quickly descended into a cesspool of sexual promiscuity, drug abuse, abortion on demand, legalized gambling, rampant blasphemy, and a flood of pornography. Our national slogan became, "If it feels good, do it!" We adopted a hedonistic lifestyle, calling evil good and good evil.

God responded by raising up prophetic voices to call the nation to repentance. One of those was Dave Wilkerson, pastor of Times Square Church in New York City. I call him

"God's Jeremiah to America." In the 70's he began writing a series of books in which he clearly outlined the sins of America and warned of judgments from God if we did not repent. Like Jeremiah, his popularity plummeted because people — even church people — did not want to hear his "doomsday message."

When the prophetic voices were ignored, God began to place remedial judgments on our nation — things like our defeat in the Vietnam War, the AIDS epidemic, the plague of sexually transmitted diseases, the scourge of homosexuality, and natural disasters in the form of monster earthquakes and killer tornados and hurricanes. We even experienced an unprecedented volcanic eruption of Mount St. Helens in 1980 — an eruption so severe that it blackened the sky from Seattle to New York City and as far south as Oklahoma.

The culmination of the remedial judgments seemed to come with the 9/11 terrorist assault in 2001 when two symbols of American pride were attacked: the Twin Towers in New York and the Pentagon in Washington, D.C. The towers stood as symbols of our wealth; the Pentagon symbolized our military power.

As I have stated before, I believe this event was a wake-up call from God for our nation to repent. Instead, like a drowsy man who doesn't want to wake-up, we merely rolled over and hit the snooze button on the alarm clock.

A New Factor

I don't think there is any doubt that our national sins have called down remedial judgments from God. But what I think we may have failed to realize is that since 1991, many of the judgments we have experienced have been directly related to our mistreatment of Israel.

The Bible says that God will bless those who bless Israel, and He will curse those who curse Israel (Genesis 12:3). The Bible also says that he who touches Israel touches "the apple of God's eye" (Zechariah 2:8).

History attests to the truth of these statements. Spain was at the height of its power as a world empire in the 15th Century when it launched the Inquisition and drove its Jewish population out of the country. Within a short time thereafter, the empire no longer existed. Hitler was well on his way to conquering all of Europe when he launched the Holocaust. His Third Reich soon ended up in ashes.

I believe that many of our blessings as a nation have been due to the fact that we have historically been a safe haven for the Jewish people. Also, we have been Israel's best friend ever since the nation came back into being in 1948.

But the Bible says that in the end times all the nations of the world will come together against Israel over the issue of Jerusalem (Zechariah 12:3). And in the early 90's we began to turn against Israel in our determination to maintain access to Arab oil.

The Decisive Year

The turning point was in 1991 when the Soviet Union collapsed and Russian Jews began flooding into Israel at the rate of 2,000 to 3,000 a day for one year. The tiny nation of Israel was overwhelmed by the refugees. The Israeli government appealed to the World Bank for a $5 billion loan. The bank said it would grant the loan only if the U. S. guaranteed it. The Bush Administration agreed to underwrite the loan on one condition: the Israelis had to go to the bargaining table and start trading land for peace.

Yes, we were the ones who forced Israel into adopting the current suicidal policy of appeasement, and we have been twisting their arm ever since, pressuring them to divide up the land which God gave them as an everlasting possession. Keep in mind that we can apply enormous pressure because our veto in the United Nations Security Council is the only thing standing between Israel and economic sanctions that could easily and quickly destroy the Israeli economy.

A Prophetic Book

In 2004 a White House correspondent (one of 250 in the world) named William Koenig wrote a book entitled, *Eye to Eye*. It was subtitled, "Facing the Consequences of Dividing Israel." The thesis of the book was that many of the natural calamities, economic setbacks, and political crises experienced by the United States since 1991 have been directly related to actions we have taken to force Israel to surrender territory to the Arabs.

Koenig is a devout Evangelical Christian who has the gift of prophecy. Accordingly, he has the discernment to see the supernatural relationship between world events and judgments of God.

His book had a very prophetic cover. It showed President Bush looking over his right shoulder at a hurricane, and in the eye of the hurricane was a Star of David, the symbol of Israel.

The title of the book, *Eye to Eye*, was suggested by Koenig's wife. She took it from Matthew Henry's commentary on Isaiah 52:8 —

> They [the watchmen] shall see an exact agreement and correspondence between the prophecy and the events, the promise and the performance; they shall see how they look upon another *eye to eye*, and be satisfied that the same God spoke the one and did the other.

In other words, in the end times there will be people who are prophetically gifted to recognize the correspondence between Bible prophecies and world events.

In his book Koenig shows the amazing parallels between U.S. mistreatment of Israel and subsequent natural calamities, economic setbacks and political crises. Let me share just a few of the examples he gives.

The Madrid Conference — This conference, which we forced on Israel, marked the beginning of the "land for peace" process. The opening of the conference on October 30, 1991, coincided with the formation of "the Perfect Storm." This was the record breaking storm along our Atlantic seacoast which produced 100 foot high waves and heavily damaged President Bush's home at Kennebunkport, Maine. The headlines of *USA Today* on November 1, 1991, had the stories of the storm and the Madrid Conference side by side.

Round Six of the Bilateral Peace Talks — In June of 1992 Yitzhak Rabin was elected the new Prime Minister of Israel. We immediately insisted that he come to Washington, D.C. and meet with Yasser Arafat. The day that meeting began, August 24, 1992, Hurricane Andrew slammed into Florida with winds of 177 miles per hour. The damage done amounted to over $30 billion — the most costly hurricane in U.S. History to that point in time.

The Camp David Summit — From July 11 through July 24 in the summer of 2000, President Clinton hosted a summit conference between Israel and the Palestinian Authority. Clinton pressured Israeli Prime Minister Ehud Barak to surrender the heartland of Israel. During these precise dates, a major heat wave struck the South Central U.S. and fires broke out in our Western states. At one point, there were over 50 active fires that consumed over 500,000 acres before the end of the month.

White House Ramadan Celebration — On Thursday evening, November 7, 2002, President Bush hosted a dinner at the White House to honor the Muslim religious holiday called Ramadan. In his speech that evening, the President said:

> . . . this season commemorates the revelation of God's word in the holy Koran to the prophet Muhammad. Today this word inspires faithful Muslims to lead lives of honesty and integrity and compassion . . .

> We see in Islam a religion that traces its
> origins back to God's call on Abraham . . .

Two days later a total of 88 tornados hit Arkansas, Tennessee, Alabama, Mississippi, Georgia, Ohio, and Pennsylvania.

The Middle East Peace Plan — On April 30, 2003, U.S. Ambassador Daniel Kurtzer presented the "Road Map" peace plan to Israeli Prime Minister Ariel Sharon. It was a plan formulated by an ungodly coalition called "the Quartet." This group was made up of Russia, the European Union, the United Nations, and the United States. It called for Israel to surrender Gaza and its heartland of Judea and Samaria to the Palestinians. On May 3rd Secretary of State Colin Powell departed for the Middle East for talks to implement the plan. On May 4th Secretary Powell met with terrorist leader Hafez Assad of Syria and made a commitment to him to include the surrender of the Golan Heights in the peace plan. That day a swarm of tornados began tearing apart the Central United States. Over the next 7 days, there was a total of 412 tornados — the largest cluster ever observed by NOAA since it began its record keeping in 1950. The previous record had been 177 in 1999.

The Sobering Summary

In summary, between October 1991 and November 2004, the United States experienced:

- 9 of the 10 largest insurance events in U.S. history.

- 9 of the 10 greatest natural disasters as ranked by FEMA relief costs.

- 5 of the costliest hurricanes in U.S. history.

- 3 of the 4 largest tornado swarms in U.S. history.

All of which were linked to our attempts to pressure Israel into either dividing up its land or surrendering part of its capital city of Jerusalem.

The world would laugh and call these coincidences, but I don't believe in coincidence. I believe only in God-incidences. God is sovereign. He is in control.

The Gaza Withdrawal

The most chaotic event in modern day Israel was the forced withdrawal of all Jews from Gaza that occurred during the late summer of 2005. It began on August 7th and continued through the 22nd, as nearly 9,000 Israelis were uprooted from their land and homes. Many had been in the area for as long as 35 years.

It was a heart-wrenching event to watch women and children manhandled, synagogues violated, torah scrolls desecrated, houses bulldozed, graves dug up, and farms destroyed. Entire Jewish communities were forcibly removed from land which God has given to the Jewish people as an everlasting possession (Psalm 105:8-11).

The economic impact on the Israeli economy was overwhelming. The farms in Gaza represented 70% of Israel's organic produce, 60% of the nation's exported herbs, 15% of its total agricultural exports, 60% of its exported cherry tomato crop, and $120 million of its flower exports.

And while this travesty was taking place, Secretary of State Condoleezza Rice began applying more pressure with the following statement: "Everyone empathizes with what the Israelis are facing . . . but it cannot be Gaza only."

The Supernatural Response

The withdrawal ended on August 22nd, and on the very next day, the government of Bermuda announced that a tropical depression had formed off its coast. Dubbed "Katrina," the storm quickly developed into the most powerful hurricane in modern history. It slammed into New Orleans and the Mississippi coast four days later on the 27th. The hurricane disrupted 25% of our crude oil production and destroyed our nation's largest port (the 5th largest in the world in terms of tonnage).

Most hurricanes take at least two weeks to develop as they come across the Atlantic Ocean and hit our eastern seaboard or as they sweep down into the Caribbean and then up into the Gulf of Mexico. Katrina, which proved to be our most powerful and devastating hurricane, developed its full strength in only five days. This had to be a supernatural storm.

I think it is interesting to note that the hurricane hit just three days before New Orleans — which often refers to itself proudly as "Sin City USA" — was scheduled to host an ungodly event that had come to be called "The Gay Mardi Gras." The theme was to be "Jazz and Jezebels." The previous year, in 2004, the event drew 125,000 revelers who proudly flaunted their perversion publicly in a parade that featured the bizarre. Incredibly, this event is sponsored by a group that has named itself "Southern Decadence."

New Orleans is known for its occult practices, particularly voodoo. The city is also infamous for its high murder rate and its rampant political corruption.

Nonetheless, I do not believe the storm was meant primarily as a judgment upon the city of New Orleans. Rather, I think it was a judgment on our entire nation for our mistreatment of Israel. The consequences of the storm were national in scope. It resulted in higher fuel prices which led to higher prices for all goods. It disrupted indefinitely the flow of goods into and out of our country. It resulted in a significant increase in our national debt. It shamed us before the world as we mishandled the aftermath. And it deeply scarred the Bush Administration.

The Impact of Theology

Speaking of President Bush, many kept asking why such a committed Evangelical would put such inordinate pressure on Israel. More and more, people asked, "Why doesn't President

Bush see the prophetic significance of end time Israel?" I put that question to Bill Koenig when I interviewed him on my television program, "Christ in Prophecy." His response was very illuminating.

Koenig pointed out that President Bush was raised in the Episcopal Church and that shortly before he became president, he started attending the Methodist Church. Although there are pastors in both of these churches who recognize the prophetic significance of modern Israel, the vast majority of the spiritual leaders in both churches (and especially those on the national level) believe in Replacement Theology. This is the theology that says God washed His hands of the Jewish people in the First Century and replaced Israel with the Church. They therefore see no prophetic significance to the re-establishment of Israel.

Koenig stated that within the Bush Administration the President was not the only victim of this erroneous theology. He asserted that the President was surrounded by godly people who had also grown up spiritually in Replacement churches. So, even though these people may have had respect for the Judaic roots of their faith, they had no appreciation for the prophetic significance of modern day Israel.

The Message of Katrina

I believe the message of Katrina is that God is on His throne. He is in control. He cannot be mocked. He will not tolerate the division of His Holy Land. Nor will He tolerate gross immorality that mocks everything that is moral and decent.

As I keep repeating over and over, God loves our nation. He has blessed us more than any other nation. But His Word says that to those to whom much is given, much is expected (Luke 12:47-48). His Word also says He disciplines those whom He loves (Hebrews 12:7).

Another thing His Word makes clear is that when He sends discipline, the fundamental purpose is never to punish. Instead, the purpose is to call us to repentance so that we might be saved. Here's how the prophet Isaiah expressed it: "When the earth experiences Your judgments, the inhabitants of the world learn righteousness" (Isaiah 26:9b).

A Personal Experience

I know the truth of this statement first-hand. In May of 1953 when I was 15 years old, an F5 tornado hit my hometown of Waco, Texas. To this day it is the most deadly tornado in Texas history. It killed 114 people and injured 597. It ripped through the center of the downtown area and leveled five story buildings with ease. When it was over, the city looked like it had been hit with an atomic bomb.

For three months thereafter, the churches of Waco were packed with standing room only crowds as people sought to cope with the tragedy. People were forced to think about eternity. But gradually the pain subsided, people returned to their old ways, and church attendance fell off.

Our God is truly a God of amazing grace. Even when He pours out His wrath, He does so hoping that it will provoke repentance so that people can be saved.

Attempts to Respond Spiritually

The Governor of Louisiana, Kathleen Blanco, called for a statewide day of prayer: "As we face the devastation wrought by Katrina, as we search for those in need, as we comfort those in pain, and as we begin the long task of rebuilding, we turn to God for strength, hope, and comfort."

Noble words. But notice, there was no call to repentance.

In like manner, President Bush called for a national day of prayer on September 8th. He asked the nation to pray for the victims and to reach out to them in compassion. Again, noble words, but no expression of repentance.

New Orleans City Council President Oliver Thomas came the closest of all public officials in recognizing that Katrina had a spiritual message. Referring to Sodom and Gomorrah, he said, "Maybe God is cleansing us."

But cleansing requires a response of repentance, something God is calling for from the whole nation, and not just the citizens of New Orleans.

The Proper Response

No public official in our nation has yet seen the spiritual implications of a disaster as clearly as did Abraham Lincoln when he evaluated the cause of the Civil War. As I pointed out on page 39, the President called for "a national day of prayer and humiliation." He began the proclamation by observing: "It is the duty of nations as well as men to own their dependence upon the overruling power of God, to confess their sins and transgressions, in humble sorrow, yet with assured hope that genuine repentance will lead to mercy and pardon."

He then went to the heart of the matter by asserting that "We have forgotten God." Instead of being thankful to God for our great blessings, Lincoln charged that "we have vainly imagined, in the deceitfulness of our hearts, that all these blessings were produced by some superior wisdom and virtue of our own."

Lincoln boldly proclaimed that the Civil War was a "punishment inflicted upon us, for our presumptuous sins." He concluded the proclamation by calling on the American people "to humble ourselves before the offended Power, to confess our national sins, and to pray for clemency and forgiveness."

How we need such a proclamation today! The sad thing is that we have become so secular and pagan that if our President were to issue such a statement, members of Congress would probably bring impeachment proceedings against him for "violation of the separation of church and state."

A Call to Prayer

We as a nation have set our jaw against God. We are tempting Him to move us from judgment to destruction. Our God is so merciful. He is patiently sending us one wake-up call after another because He never pours out His wrath without warning.

The handwriting is on the wall. Are we going to pay attention to it?

America the Beautiful?
The United States in Bible Prophecy

2009

Hail Columbia!
(First Verse)

Hail Columbia, happy land!
Hail, ye heroes, heav'n-born band,
Who fought and bled in freedom's cause,
Who fought and bled in freedom's cause,
And when the storm of war was gone
Enjoy'd the peace your valor won.
Let independence be our boast,
Ever mindful what it cost,
Ever grateful for the prize,
Let its altar reach the skies.

Chorus

Firm, united let us be,
Rallying round our liberty,
As a ban of brothers joined,
Peace and safety we shall find.

This song was the unofficial national anthem of the United States until it was replaced in 1931 when Congress adopted "The Star Spangled Banner."

Columbia is a poetic name for the United States that was used during the 18th Century. The anthem was composed by Philip Phile in 1789 for the inauguration of George Washington. It was originally titled "The President's March." Words for the music were written in 1798 by Joseph Hopkinson.

The song was used as the nation's national anthem throughout the 19th Century, but it lost popularity early in the 20th Century, after World War I. It is now used as the official song for introduction of the Vice President, in a similar fashion as "Hail to the Chief" is used for the President.

Chapter 6

The Ominous Year of 2008:
Were we delivered to destruction?

"The Lord is slow to anger and great in power, and the Lord will by no means leave the guilty unpunished."— Nahum 1:3

The Administration of President George W. Bush began in January 2001 with great hope among Evangelical Christians.

He was, after all, a born again Christian committed to strong moral values. He was opposed to abortion, and he had rejected the homosexual political agenda.

In domestic policy he had presented himself as a conservative who was committed to fiscal responsibility. He had also pledged to appoint strong conservatives to the Supreme Court.

In foreign affairs he had promised to deal strongly with terrorism and to provide continuing support for Israel.

Furthermore, he was a man of personal integrity, and there were great expectations that he would restore dignity to the office of the President.

Many of these hopes were fulfilled over the next eight years. The President stood strong against abortion and same-sex marriage. The Administration was not tainted by corruption.

When the 9/11 attacks occurred, the President showed strong leadership against terrorism. His decision to take the fight to the terrorists in Afghanistan convinced our enemies that he meant business, and the result was seven years without another major terrorist attack.

His decision to invade Iraq was controversial, but again it showed strong and determined leadership. Unlike the spineless leaders of Britain and Europe who refused to deal decisively with Hitler in the 1930's, President Bush decided to put an end to Saddam Hussein's totalitarian regime before he could become a threat to world peace.

Evangelicals could also be thankful for President Bush's outstanding appointments to the Supreme Court. Just as he had promised, Bush appointed solid conservatives who respected the Constitution and opposed judicial activism.

Areas of Weakness

There were areas of great weakness in the Bush Administration. For one thing, the President seemed unwilling to deal with illegal immigration by securing our borders. Throughout his administration, illegal immigrants continued to pour into the country, undermining the rule of law, putting great financial pressure on local governments, and causing mounting dissatisfaction with the ineptness of government among American tax payers.

Bush also fell short when it came to the details of administration. Once we had won the ground victory in Iraq, there seemed to be no follow-up plan whatsoever. We simply floundered around without any clear direction while the whole society fell apart. And the same was true of the response to Hurricane Katrina. The incompetent handling of that terrible disaster left the President and his assistants looking like a bunch of fools.

One of the President's greatest weaknesses was in the realm of communication. He surely will go down in history as one of the most inarticulate leaders of the past 100 years. He seemed incapable of justifying any of his policies, and he was never able to articulate a vision for our nation.

Policy Failures

But the two greatest failings of the Bush Administration —
the ones that were to have the greatest impact in the long run
— were related to the national debt and Israel.

During Bush's eight years in office, he allowed the national
debt to get out of control. It soared from 5.5 trillion to over 10
trillion! Some of this was due to the war effort in Iraq and
Afghanistan ($500 billion). But much of it was due to his
unwillingness to use his veto power to get spending under
control. Instead, he stood on the sidelines and watched as the
Republicans in Congress mimicked their Democrat colleagues
by feeding at the trough like a bunch of wild hogs.

The President's greatest failure was his decision to continue
imposing upon Israel a policy of appeasement with regard to
its Arab enemies. George W simply picked up where Clinton
left off, attempting to strong-arm Israel into giving up its
heartland to its enemy. It was a policy first implemented by
his father at the Madrid Conference in 1991. In the process, he
became the first President to call for the establishment of a
Palestinian state. From that point on, his Administration was
doomed, for Joel 3:2 states that God will exercise severe
judgment against any nation that tries to divide the land of
Israel in the end times.

Abandoning Israel

Evidently President Bush decided early on to push for the
establishment of a Palestinian state. On October 2, 2001 the
Associated Press reported that the President had told a meeting
of Congressional leaders that "the idea of a Palestinian state
has always been a part of a vision, so long as the right to an
Israeli state is respected."

The *New York Times* has since revealed that this decision
was made before the 9/11 attacks and that the plan was for
Secretary of State Colin Powell to announce it at the meeting
of the United Nations General Assembly scheduled for

November. The White House had also decided before September 11 that Mr. Bush would meet the Palestinian leader, Yasser Arafat, during the United Nations gathering in New York. White House correspondent, Bill Koenig, has pointed out that on the very day that Bush made his comment to Congressional leaders, the anthrax terrorist attack broke out, ultimately costing our nation billions of dollars through the destabilization of government offices for months.

A month later, on November 10, the President personally delivered his endorsement of a Palestinian state to the United Nations. He said, "The American government also stands by its commitment to a just peace in the Middle East. We are working toward the day when two states — Israel and Palestine — live peacefully together within secure and recognized borders as called for by the Security Council resolutions." Koenig observes that in that same month, the energy giant Enron reported a $638 million loss and a $1.2 billion reduction in shareholder equity. In early December it filed for Chapter 11 bankruptcy, revealing the biggest corporate fraud scandal in U. S. history up to that time.

Eight months later, on June 24, 2002, President Bush read a detailed policy statement in the Rose Garden concerning the Middle East. In it he once again affirmed his belief that a Palestinian state must be created in the heartland of Israel. The next day the second corporate bombshell hit the nation when it was revealed that the telecom giant, WorldCom, was teetering on the brink of bankruptcy after having disguised nearly $4 billion of expenses as capital expenditures to make the company appear more profitable.

The Road Map

Despite the calamities that accompanied each of these steps away from support of Israel, the President continued to put pressure on the Israeli government to surrender the heartland of its nation. His detailed policy speech of June 2002 marked the launching of what came to be known as "The Road Map to

Peace." It was a joint effort of the United States, Russia, the European Union and the United Nations. The goal was to carve a Palestinian state out of the heartland of Israel in return for a Palestinian commitment to democratic reforms and an abandonment of terrorism.

The President seemed oblivious to the fact that Arab promises have historically proved meaningless and that the Arab goal has always been the annihilation of Israel. He also refused to heed warnings given to him by many different sources that the Bible says that God will deal harshly with those who try to divide the land of Israel in the end times (Joel 3:2).

He pressured Israel to surrender the Gaza Strip in the summer of 2005, resulting in the Hurricane Katrina disaster. And up to his final months in office, he continued to apply all the pressure he could muster to get Israel to agree to the establishment of a Palestinian state before he left office.

Economic Disaster

The Lord's final response came on September 29, 2009 when the stock market crashed. The Dow Jones dropped 777 points, representing a loss of 7%, or over 1 trillion dollars.

I say it was "the Lord's response" because of two factors. First, the drop was 777 points. Second, it occurred on the eve of Rosh Hashanah, the Jewish New Year.

In the Bible the number of Man is 6, since that was the day God created Adam. The number of the Antichrist is given as 666 in Revelation 13:18 because it represents Man exalted to the utmost. It also represents the fact that during the Tribulation, a Satanic trinity will be here on earth: Satan (the fake god), the Antichrist (the fake Messiah), and the False Prophet (the fake Holy Spirit). In contrast, the number 7 in the Bible represents completed perfection because it was on the seventh day that God rested after completing His perfect Creation. Thus, 777 represents absolute perfection and can thus symbolize the true Trinity of the Father, Son and Holy Spirit.

The timing of the crash, on the eve of the Jewish New Year, seemed to me to be God's way of emphasizing the connection between the calamity and our nation's unjust treatment of Israel. It was reminiscent of the timing of Hurricane Katrina, a storm that formed the day after the Israeli withdrawal from Gaza had concluded — a withdrawal we had forced on Israel.

Looking Back

In 2003 when I wrote the first edition of this book, I outlined a number of possible scenarios that could result in the destruction of this nation and its sudden elimination as a major power in the end times, thus accounting for the silence about the United States in end time Bible prophecy (see pages 103 through 106). The scenarios included an economic collapse, an external nuclear attack, and internal terrorist attack, and internal moral rot.

In recent years another possible scenario has gained increasing attention. It is called an electromagnetic pulse attack, or EMP attack, for short.

A Serious New Threat to America

What makes this new threat so dangerous is that a relatively undeveloped country like North Korea or Iran could cripple the entire United States with the explosion of only one nuclear device in outer space, if exploded above the center of our nation. All our enemy would need is one nuclear bomb and an intercontinental ballistic missile. Or, the device could be delivered on a smaller missile launched from a merchant ship off our coasts.

The electromagnetic radiation from the explosion of a nuclear device in outer space has the potential to disrupt, if not permanently damage, all electrical grids and electronic devices. The most vulnerable are semiconductor based devices like computer chips.

The fact that an electromagnetic pulse is produced by a nuclear explosion has been known since the earliest days of atomic testing, but the magnitude of the EMP and the significance of its effects were realized slowly. Scientists began to pay serious attention to the destructive potential of EMP after a nuclear test in July of 1962 when a 1.44 megaton bomb was detonated in space above the mid-Pacific Ocean. This explosion, called the Starfish Prime Test, caused electrical damage in Hawaii, more than 800 miles from the detonation point. Later calculations showed that if the warhead had been detonated over the northern continental United States, the magnitude of the EMP would have been much larger because of the greater strength of the earth's magnetic field in that area.

Public Consciousness

The larger scientific community did not become aware of the destructive potential of EMP until 1981 when William J. Broad, the science correspondent for the *New York Times*, published a series of three articles in *Science* magazine. In 2001 the United States Congress authorized the establishment of an EMP Commission to study the significance of the threat and what could be done about it. In 2008 the Commission released its report, and it was a sobering one.

The chairman of the Commission, Dr. William R. Graham, stated that the U.S. is vulnerable to "catastrophic consequences" from a nuclear EMP attack. Beyond blackouts and communication disruptions, Graham stated that the attack would result in the failure of America's financial system and the distribution system for food and water. Graham also warned that a paralyzing EMP attack could be launched from a freighter off the U.S. coast, using a short or medium range missile. He concluded by noting that recovery from such an attack could take months to years, depending on the electronic system affected.

EMP Destructive Potential

A nuclear EMP attack would not directly harm people in the same manner as a traditional atomic attack. People would not be killed or burned by the blast. However, those with electrical implants like pacemakers would be immediately affected. Radiation sickness would be minimized by the fact that an efficient EMP explosion must take place in outer space, about 100 to 300 miles above the surface of the earth. The greatest harm people would experience would be secondary in nature, due to the collapse of electrical systems.

One nuclear device exploded 300 miles above the central United States could affect the entire country in a catastrophic manner. Hal Lindsey has summed it up as follows:

> An EMP attack . . . would overnight send the most technically developed nation back to the middle of the 19th Century. All our electrical grids would be destroyed. There would be no communications by satellite, TV, radios, telephones; no transportation as we know it, no water, no fuel, no electricity, no food, no stoves, no heat, no air-conditioning, no functioning hospitals, no elevators, no law and order, no computers, no banks, very little work force. In addition, there would be very few military weapons systems that would work.

EMP Testing

As long ago as the early 1960's the Soviet Union performed a series of EMP nuclear tests in space over Kazakhstan called "The K Project." It has recently been revealed that in May of 1999, during the NATO bombing of Yugoslavia, Russian leaders threatened a U.S. Congressional delegation with the specter of an EMP attack that would paralyze the nation.

James J. Shinn, Assistant Secretary of Defense for Asia and Pacific Security, informed the House Armed Services Committee in June 2008 that China's arms buildup includes "exotic experiments" with EMP weapons. He pointed out that the Chinese are fully aware of how heavily dependent our whole society is on sophisticated electronic communications.

In an article published in the *Jerusalem Post* in February of 2009 it was revealed that the official security journal of the Iranian government published an article in 1999 in which it identified an EMP attack "as a way to defeat the U.S. as a military power and as a state."

Dr. William Graham, in a report to the House Armed Services Committee in July 2008, stated that Iran is openly building the capacity to carry out an EMP attack. Accordingly, it is interesting that Iran described a ship-launched test of its Shihab-III missile in the Caspian Sea in 2008 as "successful" despite the fact that the missile seemed to detonate prematurely — just as would be the case with an EMP attack.

Looking Back Again

Returning to the various end time scenarios I outlined for the United States in 2003 (see pages 103 through 106), I pointed out that any of the scenarios could occur, or any combination of them, but that I felt the one that would most likely trigger the decline of our nation would be an economic collapse. Again, here's how I put it:

> I believe an unprecedented economic collapse is highly likely because money is the real god of America, and the true God of this universe is a jealous One who does not tolerate idolatry. God, by His very nature, is going to be compelled to destroy our false god. (See page 103).

One did not have to be a prophet to make such a prediction. As I pointed out at that time, our nation — both our government and our people — had become a debt junkie.

Compounding the Problem

In the six years since that time, we have continued to pile up a mountain of debt. Today, we are literally drowning in debt. The outstanding public debt of the federal government (before the Obama Stimulus Package) exceeds $11 trillion, making each citizens' share a whopping $35,070. But that is only the debt of the federal government. Private debt (household, business, and financial sectors) totals over $42 trillion. Our total debt, public and private, now stands at $53 trillion, which represents $175,154 per person.

Most household debt consists primarily of a mortgage, auto loans, and balances due on credit cards. Mortgage debt is the largest item. In March of 2008 the equity existing in all mortgage loans was estimated to be only 5.5%, meaning that mortgage loans were leveraged 18 times on average. Since that time, as housing prices have plummeted dramatically due to the subprime scandal, the supporting equity ratio has also declined to the lowest in recorded history.

Meanwhile, the average auto loan today is 63 months, with some extending to as many as 80 months. I can remember in the late 1950's when the maximum length of a car loan was 24 months, and a down payment of one-third was required.

And then there is our massive credit card debt. When I graduated from college in 1959, the first general-use credit card had just been introduced — the BankAmericard (which later became Visa). I tried to get one for convenience purposes, but I was rejected even though I had no outstanding debt. Today, when freshmen college students arrive on campus for classes, the credit card companies have displays enticing them to sign up for a credit card and then give them free gifts for doing so. The result is that 76% of undergraduates now have credit cards, and the average undergrad has $2,200 in credit card debt.

Overall, over 150 million Americans have credit cards, and each of these has an average of nine cards, meaning there are almost 1.5 billion cards in circulation. What is particularly disturbing is the fact that almost 45% of credit card holders are making just minimum payment or no payments at all on their credit card balances. The result is that the average American household in 2008 carried nearly $8,700 in credit card debt.

One expert on American debt, Michael Hodges, has summed up the situation in these words: "America has become less a family-based, frugal and productive society with small government — and more a consumptive, permissive, debt-dependent and government-driven society than ever."

The Obama Plunge

Now we have added a trillion dollars to our national debt overnight with the passage of the Obama Stimulus Package. Even more alarming, the Obama Administration has become the first government in human history to propose a one trillion dollar debt in its regular budget, and the President has stated that we can expect a trillion dollars in additional debt each year "as far as the eye can see into the future."

It is almost impossible for our minds to grasp the size of such a debt. One trillion seconds of time equals 31,546 years, so if you were to spend one dollar per second, it would take 31,546 years to spend one trillion dollars.

It is madness to believe that we can solve our debt problem by amassing more debt. Who has ever spent their way out of debt? Of course, the U. S. government can do something that we as private citizens cannot do — it can print money. And as we do that, we will dig our own grave. The stimulus spending may produce a temporary upswing, but it will ultimately result in a hyper-inflation that will wipe out life savings overnight.

In the 20th Century the god of our nation became the Almighty Dollar. Motivated by an insatiable greed, we began worshiping at its altar. And now we must pay the price for our idolatry — namely, the destruction of our economy.

Political Disaster

This brings us to the second great disaster of 2008. The first was the stock market crash in September. The second was the election of Barack Obama in November.

Obama was considered to be the most liberal member of the United States Senate. He is, in fact, a liberal ideologue who is the most pro-abortion, pro-homosexual, anti-Capitalist, anti-Israel president in our history. Even more alarming, he is a Christian in name only.

Obama's Kenyan father and Indonesian step-father were both Muslims, but there is little evidence that he was ever indoctrinated into the Muslim faith. He claims his American mother was a Christian, but he says they went to church only once a year on Easter. In his autobiography, *The Audacity of Hope*, he states point-blank, "I was not raised in a religious household."

In March of 2004, right after he had secured the Democrat nomination for the U.S. Senate in Illinois, Obama sat down with *Chicago Times* columnist, Cathleen Flasani, and gave her an in-depth interview about his religious faith. In it he revealed that he never had any real involvement in Christianity until 1985 when a group of Chicago churches banded together to deal with unemployment in their neighborhoods. They hired Obama to work for them as a community organizer. It was then that he got involved with Trinity United Church of Christ and its pastor, Jeremiah Wright. In 1987 he joined the church and began to profess that he was a Christian.

But claiming to be a Christian does not make a person a Christian. As the syndicated columnist Cal Thomas has put it, "Obama can call himself anything he likes, but there is a clear requirement for one to qualify as a Christian, and Obama doesn't meet that requirement. One cannot deny central tenents of the Christian faith, including the deity and uniqueness of Christ as the sole mediator between God and Man and be a Christian."

A Revealing Interview

Obama made it very clear in his 2004 interview with Cathleen Flasani that he does not believe the central tenets of the Christian faith. For example, he stated point-blank, "I believe there are many paths to the same place [Heaven]." Yet Jesus stated in John 14:6 that "I am the way and the truth and the life. No one comes to the Father except through me."

When Flasani asked Obama, "Who's Jesus to you?" he responded that Jesus was an "historical figure," a "bridge between God and Man," and "a wonderful teacher." There was no expression of Jesus as God in the flesh, the Savior who died for our sins.

When asked if he prayed often, Obama said he did, but he added, "It's not formal, me getting on my knees. I think I have an ongoing conversation with God. I think throughout the day. I'm constantly asking myself questions about what I'm doing, why I am doing it." In other words, Obama prays to himself!

Obama's Difficulty with Christianity

Obama also admitted that there was one thing in particular about Christianity that he has difficulty dealing with and that is the tendency of many Christians to engage in evangelism! He said he believed this desire to proselytize was based on a belief that if "people haven't embraced Jesus Christ as their personal Savior, that they're going to Hell." Obama has obviously never heard of the Great Commandment to preach the Gospel to all the world (Mark 16:15-16).

Flasani was so shocked by this statement, that she replied, "You don't believe that?" Obama's response was, "I find it hard to believe that my God would consign four-fifths of the world to Hell."

She then asked Obama if he believed in Heaven, to which he replied, "I don't presume to have knowledge of what happens after I die." He added, "What I believe is that if I live my life as well as I can, that I will be rewarded." In short, his faith is in his own good works, the very antitheses of Christianity and its teaching that salvation is by grace through faith, apart from works (Ephesians 2:8-9).

Flasani concluded her remarkable interview of Obama by asking him to give her a role model that would summarize his faith. He immediately pointed to Gandhi and then added Dr. Martin Luther King and President Abraham Lincoln to the list.

Joseph Farah, the editor of WorldNetDaily, summarized this interview by observing that Obama's comments make it clear that "he doesn't have a clue as to what it means to be a Christian."

From Judgment to Destruction

In the first edition of this book in 2003, I stated that one of the remedial judgments that God often places on a nation is that He gives the people the kind of leaders they deserve (see page 30). Can there be any doubt that this is precisely what He has done to the United States? Since the 1960's our nation has been caught up in rebellion against God. We cannot kill babies in their mother's wombs, promote same-sex marriage, produce filthy movies and TV programs, worship the dollar, and pressure Israel to give up its heartland and expect God to continue to bless us.

He has called us to repentance through prophetic voices and remedial judgments, and we have turned our backs on both. In chapter 1 (see page 41) I pointed out that one of the principles that guides God's relationship with a nation is that He will destroy it when the nation's rebellion reaches the point of no return — what the Bible calls the point at which "your wound becomes incurable" (Nahum 3:19 and Jeremiah 30:12).

I believe 2008 may prove to be the year that God decided to deliver us from judgment to destruction, first by critically weakening our economy and then by supplying us with a pagan Humanist as our President.

Obama's Attack on Christian Values

That Obama represents a scourge on our nation became clear as soon as he took the oath of office, for he wasted no time in declaring war on Evangelical Christianity. Within minutes, his staff posted on the White House website his agenda concerning homosexuality and abortion.

With regard to sexual perversion, the President's policy goals are spelled out as follows:

1) Defeat all state and federal constitutional efforts to defend the definition of biblical marriage as being a union between one man and one woman.

2) Repeal the Defense of Marriage Act (DOMA) signed by Bill Clinton. (This is currently the only line of defense keeping all 50 states from being forced to recognize so-called "same-sex marriages" from extremely liberal states like Massachusetts and Connecticut.)

3) Repeal the military's "Don't Ask, Don't Tell" policy.

4) Pass "hate crimes" legislation granting homosexuals and cross dressers special rights denied to other Americans. (This legislation, depending on how it is drafted, could even attempt to muzzle any criticism of homosexuality as being unbiblical and an unnatural perversion.)

5) Pass the Employment Non-Discrimination Act (ENDA) which would force business owners (religious and otherwise) to abandon traditional values relative to sexual morality under penalty of law.

6) Create intentionally motherless and fatherless homes by expanding "gay adoption."

The Sanctity of Life

With regard to abortion, the White House website outlines the President's agenda as follows:

1) Opposition to any constitutional amendment to overturn the Supreme Court's abortion decision in Roe v Wade.

2) Support of the Prevention First Act which would provide access to contraception and "preventive services to help reduce unintended pregnancies" (a euphemism for abortion).

Although it is not mentioned on the website, the President has made it clear that he will support the Freedom of Choice Act (FOCA). In fact, he promised Planned Parenthood that signing the FOCA would be "the first thing I'd do as President." FOCA is by far the most radical piece of abortion legislation ever introduced into the Congress.

According to pro-choice advocates:

- FOCA would overturn the ban on the barbaric procedure called "partial-birth abortion."

- FOCA would invalidate scores of pro-life laws passed by dozens of states.

- FOCA would eliminate existing laws against taxpayer funded abortions.

This outrageous attack on biblical morals should come as no surprise to anyone. The American voters were warned time and time again during the presidential campaign that Obama would push the most radical homosexual and abortion agenda in American history. But millions voted for race, charisma or eloquence rather than paying attention to the issues.

The Fate of Our Nation

There is no way to overemphasize how critical a situation we are facing in this country. The fate of our nation hangs in the balance. We are in the midst of a great financial crisis and we have enemies worldwide who desire to destroy us. I want to see President Obama succeed in solving our financial crisis and defending this nation against Islamic terrorism. But he has literally no hope of succeeding as long as he thumbs his nose at God and God's Word.

In addition to pushing homosexuality, same-sex marriage, and abortion, Obama has also made it clear that he will demand a division of the land of Israel as part of a "two-state solution."

These policies are national suicide.

Equally disturbing is Obama's seeming blindness to the threat of Islamic fundamentalism. One of his first actions as President was to announce the closing of the terrorist prison at Guantanamo Bay. The first foreign political leader he called was Mahmoud Abbas, the President of the Palestinian Authority. He then announced that he was going to provide aid to pay the cost for refugees in Gaza to immigrate to the United States, despite the fact that all of these people are Hamas supporters or sympathizers. And then he sent the new Secretary of State, Hillary Clinton, to the Middle East to offer the Palestinians $900 million in relief aid. Based on past experience, this money will either end up in private bank accounts or else be spent on arms to be used against Israel.

Meanwhile, he continued to announce his intention to begin diplomatic negotiations with both Iran and the Taliban. This major change in policy is a clear indication that as a committed Humanist, he believes in the basic goodness of Man and therefore believes he can find a political settlement to all problems, if we are only willing to compromise. Again, he seems to be blind to the fact that there are truly evil people who are determined to destroy both us and Israel, and their ideology prohibits them from making any compromises except for temporary convenience.

A Call to Prayer

God cannot be mocked, nor can He be deceived (Galatians 6:7). He will not sit idly by and allow our nation to turn its back on Him and wallow in immorality. Nor will He allow us to sell out Israel for Arab acceptance and access to their oil. We have been blessed more mightily than any other nation in history, and to those to whom much is given, much is expected (Luke 12:47-48).

We need to pray as we have never prayed before for our President. We need to pray for him to come to know God's Word and the Savior revealed by that Word. We need to pray for his heart to be softened and his ideas to be conformed to God's Word (Proverbs 21:1). And we need to pray that all his efforts to implement policies contrary to God's Word will be confused, frustrated, and defeated.

Chapter 7

International Stage-Setting:
Is the Tribulation near?

"The Lord of hosts has planned, and who can frustrate it? And as for His stretched out hand, who can turn it back?" Isaiah 14:27

While the United States disintegrates before our very eyes, other areas of the world are experiencing revival in accordance with end time prophecies. It is important for us to take a look at these developments because they relate to the ultimate fate of our nation.

The European Phoenix

The 21st Century has continued to witness one of the greatest miracles of modern times regarding the nations of the world, one that is second only to the re-establishment of Israel. That, of course, is the coalescing of Europe into a revival of the old Roman Empire, just as Daniel prophesied would happen over 2,500 years ago.

As planned, the European Union added ten new members in May of 2004, bringing the total membership to 25 nations. The addition of these new members required some adjustments of the internal voting systems and an enlargement of the European Parliament from 626 seats to 732. These changes were agreed to in the Treaty of Nice which was signed in 2001 and came into effect in 2003.

On January 1, 2007, two additional states — Romania and Bulgaria — became members, bringing the total membership to 27 nations. Croatia, Macedonia, and Turkey are currently negotiating to become members. The attempts of Norway and Switzerland to gain membership have been voted down in national referendums.

The EU is based upon a series of very complex treaties — the Treaty of Rome (1957), the Maastricht Treaty (1993), the Treaty of Amsterdam (1999), and the Nice Treaty (2003). To clarify these treaties and to provide a more substantial political structure for the EU, a European Constitution was drafted and signed by all the member nations in Rome in October of 2004. Its full implementation was dependent upon its ratification by all the member states, several of whom decided to submit it to national referendums.

The Constitution was intended to provide the EU for the first time with a "legal personality." This meant it would be able to represent itself as a single body under international law, thus being able, for example, to sign treaties for all the member states. It was also designed to streamline the structure, increase the power of the Parliament, and create some important new leadership positions.

A Shocking Setback

But to the astonishment of the EU leadership, two key nations refused to approve the Constitution in public referendums. They were France and the Netherlands. Since the Constitution required unanimous approval, it was placed on hold for what was called "a period of reflection."

In March of 2007 the three key leaders of the EU — the presiding officers of the Parliament, the Council and the Commission — ended this period with the signing of a document called the Berlin Declaration. This document was intended to provide renewed impetus toward the breaking of the ratification deadlock. It called for a solution to the problem to be reached before the European Parliament elections scheduled for June of 2009.

The Treaty of Lisbon

In December of 2007 the European Council agreed to drop the proposed Constitution, but to retain most of its changes in the form of another treaty called the Treaty of Lisbon. This treaty increases the power of the European Parliament in the legislative process (which has been dominated by the European Council); creates a High Representative for Foreign Affairs; and makes the EU Human Rights Charter legally binding on all the member states.

Perhaps the most important change from a biblical viewpoint is the fact that the treaty creates a new kind of president of the Council, the EU's most powerful body. In the past this position has been held by the head of government of the state chairing the Council, with rotation every six months. The Treaty of Lisbon would create a president elected by the heads of state to serve for a term of 2½ years. This prestigious new position is being referred to in European newspapers as "The President of Europe." Currently Tony Blair, the former Prime Minister of Great Britain, is jockeying for the position. It is this position that the future Antichrist is most likely to hold.

Another Setback

Although the Treaty of Lisbon basically constitutes the defeated constitution, since it is in the form of a treaty, all the member states decided to ratify it by parliamentary votes rather than public referendums. All, that is, except Ireland. The Irish decided they were compelled by a 1987 decision of their Supreme Court to submit the treaty to a public referendum. The election was held in June of 2008, and the Irish rejected the treaty. Since the implementation of the treaty depends on unanimous ratification, it is currently in suspension, waiting either on another Irish vote or a renegotiating process.

Thus far, the EU leaders have refused to renegotiate the treaty. They have talked the Irish into conducting another election by November of 2009 on the condition that they will provide some legal guarantees that certain EU rules concerning "family issues" will not be imposed upon Ireland. These include abortion, euthanasia and gay marriage. They have also agreed to allow the Irish to retain their traditional state neutrality. Meanwhile, both Poland and the Czech Republic have held up their ratifications pending a decision by Ireland.

The Future

The bottom line is that the leaders of the EU are determined to have their new constitution one way or another, and they will not rest until they get it ratified.

Even with the new constitution, the EU will remain a loose confederation of states for the time being. This is in conformity with end time Bible prophecy which portrays the revived Roman Empire as a mixture of iron and clay (Daniel 2:41-43). It will not become a unified political superpower until the Antichrist takes it over and consolidates it into his power base from which he will conquer the world (Revelation 13:7).

The development we should watch for is the division of the EU into ten administrative units which will cut across national boundaries, with a president heading up each of the areas. The book of Daniel says the Antichrist will rise to power within the revived Roman Empire by subduing three of these leaders and then taking over the entire organization (Daniel 7:24-25).

The Role of Turkey

The nation of Turkey applied for membership in the European Union over 20 years ago in 1987. The nation was made an "associate member in 1992, but its full membership has been held up over the years for many technical reasons.

The fundamental issue, however, has always been Turkey's Muslim culture. For many years the Turks played down this cultural difference, emphasizing the fact that after World War I, which resulted in the collapse of the Ottoman Empire, the nation's government was secularized by Kemal Ataturk.

But many in Europe have feared the addition of Turkey to the EU. For one thing, the Turkish population of over 70 million is second only to Germany among EU members, and it is most likely to surpass Germany in 2010. Even more important, if Turkey were to be admitted to full membership, Turkish workers would have the freedom to move to any nation within the EU, resulting in a flood of Muslims into the heart of Europe.

In 2003 the likelihood of Turkey ever becoming admitted to full membership in the EU became very remote, for in that year the first militant Islamic politician became Prime Minister since the state had been constitutionally secularized. He remains in power to this day.

His name is Recep Tayyip Erdogan. He is a former mayor of Istanbul, and he is a devout Sunni Muslim who seems determined to overthrow Turkey's secular constitution and replace it with Islamic Sharia law. In 1997 he was imprisoned for publicly reading a militant poem he had written:

> Mosques are our barracks/ domes our helmets/ minarets our bayonets/ believers our soldiers/ This holy army guards my religion/ Almighty, our journey is our destiny/ the end is martyrdom.

Since becoming Prime Minister, Erdogan has stated, "It is not possible to be secular and Muslim at the same time . . . The Islamic nation is waiting for the rise of the Muslim Turkish nation." This is not rhetoric designed to win the hearts of Europeans.

Although Erdogan has not withdrawn Turkey's application for membership in the EU, it appears that if he has his way, he will veer toward a closer identity with the Middle Eastern Muslim world. And this is in accordance with Bible prophecy because Ezekiel 38 says that Turkey will be one of the major allies of Russia when the Russians lead an Islamic invasion of Israel.

The Bear is Back

The Roman Empire in the form of the European Union is not the only empire rising from the dead in these end times. Russia is also revitalizing.

After the 1991 collapse of Communism in Russia, the nation was brought to its knees as it was forced to live on foreign charity to balance its books. The economy collapsed. Unemployment soared. The ruble became worthless. Stores were empty. People bartered on the streets, trading blue jeans for food, and they were reduced to yearning for the "good old days" of Stalin. They may not have had much individual freedom in those days, but they had jobs and food on the table.

By 1998 the economic situation had become so bad that the Russian government was forced to devalue the ruble by 75%. It also defaulted on more than $30 billion of loans. The country teetered on the brink of complete collapse.

The crisis forced the Yeltsin government to launch extensive economic reforms. Subsidies for inefficient state enterprises were slashed. Others were sold to private investors. Government spending was slashed, and the budget was brought back into balance.

But the true resurgence of Russia did not begin until Vladimir Putin took over as President in 2000. Putin moved quickly to implement widespread economic reforms that were anchored in substantial tax reductions. At the same time, the price of oil began to rise, going from $12 a barrel in 1998 to over $140 in 2008.

The Impact of Petro-Dollars

Since Russia is the world's second largest oil producer, this exponential rise in the price of oil produced a financial bonanza for the nation. Oil export revenue jumped dramatically from $8.8 billion in 1998 to more than $58 billion in 2004. Putin wisely decided to create a stabilization fund in 2004 as insurance against a sudden drop in oil prices. By the end of 2007 this fund contained about $160 billion.

The flood of oil money produced spectacular economic growth. Between 2000 and 2007 the nation experienced seven consecutive years of economic expansion, averaging over 6% per year. In 2007 the GDP grew 8.1%, surpassing the growth rates of all the other G8 countries. In 2008 the growth rate fell to 5.6% due to the international financial crisis and a sharp fall in oil prices. Even so, at the beginning of 2009 Russia was in relatively good financial shape with over $385 billion in foreign exchange reserves and with its oil stabilization fund to draw on.

Political Tinkering

The political side of the Russian equation was not so healthy when 2009 began. That's because Putin spent much of his time during his presidency (2000 - 2008) radically "restructuring" the political system to bolster his power. In what many called a "constitutional coup d'etat," he ended the popular election of governors and started appointing them himself.

He took over or closed all media outlets. He engineered a new electoral law that killed off all minor parties. (It has been so effective that there are only 5 opposition members among the 447 deputies in the Parliament!) He trampled on human rights with abuses that include abduction, torture, and unlawful detention. And he acquired legislation to eliminate jury trials in cases of terrorism, hostage-taking, rioting, treason, espionage, sedition, armed rebellion, and sabotage.

In 2008 Putin faced a constitutional limitation of two consecutive terms as President. He dealt with the restriction by arranging for his right hand man, Dmitry Medvedev, to succeed him. The first thing Medvedev did after being sworn in as the new President in May of 2008 was to appoint Putin as Prime Minister.

Today, Medvedev serves as the de jure head of government, but Putin is the de facto ruler. Putin can return as

President when Medvedev's term is completed in 2012, and he is currently engineering a change in the constitution to provide for a longer term.

Putin refers to the new Russian government as a "managed democracy," but it is anything except democratic. Others have characterized it as "imperial management," "Kremlin, Inc.," "a dictatorship," and "a ramshackle authoritarian system."

The best description I have run across is one by Bret Stephens in an article in the *Wall Street Journal*: "Russia has become, in the precise sense of the word, a fascist state." He proceeds to characterize Putin as a "popular despot." He concludes with this observation: "Popularity is what competent despots get when they destroy independent media, stoke nationalistic fervor with military buildups and the cunning exploitation of the Church, and ride a wave of petrodollars to pay off the civil service and balance the budget."

Imperial Designs

One thing for certain about the revived Russian government is that it is dangerous. Putin is anxious to rebuild the old Soviet Empire. He does not hesitate to bully the leaders of the former Soviet Republics, and as he demonstrated in Georgia, he is willing to resort to force when they fail to toe the line.

He is also willing to take any step necessary to halt U.S. influence in the former Soviet Republics and to limit that influence throughout the Middle East. In February 2005 he traveled to Iran to meet with its President. While there, he signed an agreement to provide fuel for Iran's new nuclear reactor in Bushehr. He took advantage of the occasion to issue a warning that he would not tolerate the territory of any Caspian nation being used for an attack on Iran. This warning was based on a concern that the U.S. might use an air base in Azerbaijan as a staging ground for military strikes in Iran. Later that year, in December, Russia signed a deal to sell an anti-missile system to Iran.

When the Russians invaded Georgia, Zbigniew Brzezinski, Jimmy Carter's former security adviser, gave an interview to *The Huffington Post* in which he observed:

> Unfortunately, Putin is putting Russia on a course that is ominously similar to Stalin's and Hitler's in the later 1930s. Swedish foreign minister Carl Bildt has correctly drawn an analogy between Putin's "justification" for dismembering Georgia — because of the Russians in South Ossetia — to Hitler's tactics vis-a-vis Czechoslovakia to "free" the Sudeten Deutsche.
>
> Even more ominous is the analogy of what Putin is doing vis-a-vis Georgia to what Stalin did vis-a-vis Finland: subverting by use of force the sovereignty of a small democratic neighbor. In effect, morally and strategically, Georgia is the Finland of our day.

Brzezinski went on to conclude that Putin has imperial designs in mind: "to reintegrate the former Soviet space under the Kremlin's control and to cut Western access to the Caspian Sea and Central Asia by gaining control over the Baku/Ceyhan pipeline that runs through Georgia."

Biblical Implications

The Russian reassertion of its dominance over Georgia is important biblically because Georgia provides the land bridge for the movement of Russian troops into the Middle East, something that will happen when the Russian-led invasion of Israel occurs, together with Iran, Turkey, and other Muslim allies (Ezekiel 38 and 39).

The lack of any response from the West except a series of diplomatic protests is also significant. The Russians have tested the water, and it was nice and warm. They have been encouraged to take the plunge.

This brings us to the cornerstone of end time Bible prophecy — the nation of Israel.

A Desperate Nation

Since the turn of the Century, Israel has moved into a critical situation. The continuing existence of the nation has become a question mark. In the natural, there appears to be no hope that the nation can survive for long.

The Jewish people have grown war-weary after 60 years of never-ending hostilities. They and their leaders seem to have lost the Zionist vision. And the noose of Arab nations around them has tightened as each of their enemies has acquired missiles which they are willing to use indiscriminately.

In their desperation for peace, the Israelis have embraced a suicidal policy of appeasement that only whets the appetite of the Arabs and encourages them to press harder for more and more Israeli capitulations.

Meanwhile, the world's major international organizations (the United Nations, the European Union, and the Vatican) are all applying intense diplomatic pressure on Israel, trying to force the nation to surrender its heartland and half of Jerusalem. And the only friend Israel has ever had — the United States — has joined the international chorus of voices demanding the creation of a Palestinian state.

The stage is set for the outbreak of a major war in the Middle East that will lead to the rise of the Antichrist and the onset of the Tribulation.

What's Next?

Most Bible prophecy experts believe that the next war will be the one prophesied in Ezekiel 38 and 39, often referred to as the War of Gog & Magog. This is an invasion of Israel by a coalition of Muslim nations led by Russia. But the problem with that expectation is that the conditions for that war do not yet exist.

For example, the passages in Ezekiel say the war will occur at a time when the Israelis are "living securely" (Ezekiel 38:8 and 38:14) "without walls" (Ezekiel 38:11). That certainly is not the case today. Not only are they living in a state of constant insecurity, but they are in the process of building a 300 mile long wall down the middle of the country to protect their nation from terrorist attacks.

A Different Theory

A new voice on the Bible prophecy scene, Bill Salus, published a book called *Isralestine* in 2008 in which he proposed the idea that the next major war in the Middle East is likely to be the one pictured in Psalm 83. Such a war would involve the immediate Arab neighbors of Israel — those with a common border. This coalition would include Lebanon, Syria, Jordan, Egypt, and Gaza. It is this war that would most likely lead to the prophesied destruction of Damascus (Isaiah 17:1-14 and Jeremiah 49:23-27).

We know for certain that if such a war were to occur, Israel would win it because of promises God has made concerning Israel in the end times. In Amos 9:15 God promised that once the Jews are regathered to their land, they will never be "rooted out" again. And in Zechariah 12:6 God promised that the revived nation of Israel would be like "a firepot among pieces of wood," consuming all the surrounding peoples.

Salus believes the Psalm 83 War will result in an overwhelming Israeli victory and will provide the peace and security for Israel that is mentioned in Ezekiel 38. Such a war would also solve another problem. The specific nations mentioned as Russian allies in Ezekiel 38 and 39 include Iran, Ethiopia, Libya and Turkey. Why is it that none of the Arab nations adjacent to Israel are mentioned? Salus believes it is because they will have already been defeated by Israel in the Psalm 83 War.

Psalm 83 Leads to Ezekiel 38

So, there is likely to be a Psalm 83 War that will result in Israel decisively defeating all its Muslim neighbors, resulting in a greatly empowered and expanded Israel living in peace. The remaining Muslim nations in the Middle East, with the exception of Saudi Arabia (the "Sheba and Dedan" of Ezekiel 38:13), would then turn to Russia for assistance. The Russians, who have always wanted the oil fields of the Middle East, will respond to the Arab pleas by launching the invasion of Israel described in Ezekiel 38 and 39. God will respond by destroying the Russian coalition supernaturally upon the mountains of Israel (Ezekiel 38:19-22 and 39:1-6).

The Psalm 83 War, which the Israelis will win with their own military power, will result in the destruction of the inner ring of Muslim states surrounding Israel. The Ezekiel 38 War will result in the supernatural destruction of the armies of Russia and the outer ring of Muslim states encircling Israel.

In the midst of the chaos produced by the Ezekiel 38 War, the Antichrist will arise out of the European Union and will negotiate a treaty with Israel that will guarantee its peace and enable the rebuilding of the Jewish Temple.

In short, we are standing today on the threshold of the Tribulation, which means, of course, that the Rapture of the Church is right around the corner.

An Additional Condition

There is one other condition of the Ezekiel 38 War that has not been met until recently. In Ezekiel 38:12-13 there is a strong implication that the Russian invasion will be motivated at least in part by a desire "to capture spoil and seize plunder."

There has been much speculation over the years as to what this spoil might be. Some have theorized it would be the mineral wealth of the Dead Sea. Others have postulated a major oil strike in Israel or the Israeli invention of a super fertilizer. I have personally always thought it was simply a reference to the Arab oil fields. In other words, I have thought the Russians would use the Arab pleas for help against Israel as a ruse to capture the oil fields of the very Arab nations appealing for help.

A recent startling development has now thrown new light on this question of spoil and plunder. On January 8, 2009 the Noble Energy Company announced that it had discovered a major gas field off the coast of Haifa estimated to be 3 trillion cubic feet in size. A month later, after further testing, the estimated size of the field was increased to 5 trillion cubic feet!

The Nuclear Threat

Meanwhile, the threat of nuclear annihilation hangs over the heads of Israelis as the President of Iran, Mahmoud Ahmadinejad, continues to threaten an atomic attack once he has secured a nuclear bomb. Israel cannot afford to ignore this threat. They must take pre-emptive action, even as they did against Iraq in 1981 when they pulled off a surprise attack on the nuclear reactor at Osirak.

When they do so, they will be condemned by the world, just as they were in 1981, despite the fact that any other nation under the same insane threat would take the same action. But the world has a double standard when it comes to Israel. So Israel will be condemned.

The strike could spark the Psalm 83 War, with Iran supplying the money and arms for Israel's neighbors to launch a barrage of missile attacks from all directions.

It is obvious that the nation of Israel is facing some difficult times. There is really no reason why the nation should survive except for the fact that "He who keeps Israel will neither slumber nor sleep" (Psalm 121:4). Two-thirds of the Jewish people are going to die in the wars that lie ahead (Zechariah 13:8-9). That is the terrible news of Bible prophecy. But the overwhelming good news of God's Prophetic Word is that those Jews who survive to the end of the Tribulation will come to the end of themselves and turn their eyes to God and accept His Son, Yeshua, as their Messiah (Zechariah 12:10 and Romans 9:27).

The Fate of the Muslims

What about Israel's Arab neighbors? What will happen to them?

The Bible prophesies that God will pour out judgment upon the Arab nations in the end times for their hostility toward the Jews and their attempt to claim the Jewish homeland as their own. Consider Joel 3:19, for example. This passage has a clear end time context, and in that context it says, "Egypt will become a waste, and Edom will become a desolate wilderness, because of the violence done to the sons of Judah, in whose land they have shed innocent blood."

Keep in mind that Edom is often used as a symbolic term for all the Arab peoples, just as Israel is used as a term for all the Jewish tribes. Ezekiel says that "all Edom" will be dealt with in the end times because of its hatred against the Jews and its lust for their land (Ezekiel 35:10-11 and 36:1-7). The result will be the desolation of the Arab states (Ezekiel 35:15). The book of Obadiah prophesies a similar fate for Edom in "the day of the Lord" (Obadiah 15-18).

Part of this destruction is going to take place in the wars of Psalm 83 and Ezekiel 38, most likely before the Tribulation begins. But these wars affect only the nations in the Middle East. The vast majority of Muslims live in nations outside the Middle East.

Tribulation Judgment

I believe the Muslims in other parts of the world, like Pakistan, Bangladesh, and Indonesia, will taste the wrath of God at the beginning of the Tribulation when they refuse to accept the European Antichrist. They will become the focus of the Antichrist's military actions to subdue all the world to his authority.

The book of Revelation states that one-fourth of humanity will die in the initial military campaign of the Antichrist (chapter 6). That's 1.5 billion people in today's terms. Then, we are told that the war will expand into what appears to be a nuclear holocaust, and during this second phase (chapters 8 and 9), one-third of those remaining will die. That's another 1.5 billion.

So, a total of 3 billion people are going to be killed in the wars of the Antichrist during the first half of the Tribulation. I believe most of those will be Muslims.

Hope for the Arabs

But the future for the Arabs is not all bleak. They must suffer for their sins just as the Jewish people will suffer during the Tribulation. And, like the Jews, a remnant of the Arabs will emerge from their suffering with their hearts turned to the one and only true God (Jeremiah 12:14-17).

The most remarkable prophecy concerning the future salvation of an Arab remnant is contained in Isaiah 19:16-25. Isaiah says that when the Lord strikes Egypt and Assyria, they will turn to Him and He will have compassion on them and "heal them." Isaiah then presents an incredible picture of Egypt, Assyria and Israel living together in peace during the Millennium, worshiping the same God!

Another remarkable prophecy concerns the Arabs who will be living in the land of Israel after the Lord returns. This prophecy relates to the fact that the territory of Israel will be greatly expanded when Jesus returns, incorporating many of the Arab nations that exist today. (The considerably expanded borders of Israel during the Millennium are detailed in Ezekiel 47:15-20.) Amazingly, Ezekiel says that the Arabs living in Israel at that time will be "allotted an inheritance" of the land together with the tribes of Israel! (Ezekiel 47:21-23. See also Isaiah 14:1-2.)

God's Love for the Arabs

The Bible says the Jewish people are the "apple of God's eye" (Zechariah 2:8), but that does not mean that He has no love for their cousins, the Arabs. Just as God has covenants with the Jews, He has a covenant with the Arab peoples. You can find it in Genesis 16:11-12 and 17:20-21. In this covenant, God promised to make the descendants of Ishmael (the Arabs) a great nation and to give them all the land to the east of their Jewish brethren.

God has been faithful to these promises. Today there are 22 Arab nations with a combined population of 289 million people. The Arabs occupy a total area of 5.3 million square miles of oil rich land. By contrast, there is only one Jewish state with a population of 5 million Jews who are squeezed into only 8 thousand square miles of space. That's a population ratio of 58 to 1 and a land ratio of 662 to 1. The Arabs have truly been blessed.

Our Impartial God

There is no partiality with God (Romans 2:11). He chose the Jews, not to be a repository of His blessings, but to be a vehicle through whom He would bless all the nations of the world, including the Arabs. But the fundamental requirement to receive God's blessings — for both Jew and Arab, as well as all people — is to accept God's gift of love in Jesus by receiving Him as Messiah.

When I consider the blessings God has given the Arab peoples and the grace He is going to show toward them in the future, despite their persecution of His Chosen People, I am reminded of what Paul wrote when he considered God's grace toward his Jewish brethren: "Oh, the depth of the riches both of the wisdom and knowledge of God! How unsearchable are His judgments and unfathomable His ways!" (Romans 11:33).

The End Time Pattern

The Bible clearly prophesies that in the end times there will be a very specific configuration of nations on the international scene.

- Israel will be re-established.

- Israel will be surrounded by hostile Arab nations intent upon its destruction.

- A nation located in the remote parts of the north (Russia) will pose a serious threat to Israel.

- Russia will be allied with Iran.

- Turkey will be allied with its Muslim neighbors.

- The Roman Empire will be revived.

- Nations will exist in Asia that are capable of raising an army of 200 million men.

- The United States will not be a key player on the international scene.

As we look on the world scene today, we can see that all of these parts of the end time international pattern are either in place or else they are in the process of coalescing.

The Disappearance of America

I have presented several scenarios to explain the sudden disappearance of the United States as a world power — an economic collapse, an external nuclear attack, an internal terrorist attack, or an EMP attack. In 2003 I stated that I felt our demise would begin with an economic collapse because money had become our god, and the true God of this universe would destroy our false god.

The economic collapse has begun. Other calamities could be added to it, and likely will be. David Wilkerson, the pastor of Times Square Church in New York City, has had repeated visions since the early 1970's about the destruction of New

York City and other major cities in our nation.

Such destruction could result from any of the scenarios I have described, or any combination of them. It could also be the result of the event that I think will seal our fate — namely, the Rapture of the Church.

As we look to the future, is there any hope for America? Is our fate really sealed? Have we reached the point where our wound is incurable?

Chapter 8

The Only Hope for America:
What is it?

"The angel of the Lord encamps around those who fear Him, and rescues them." Psalm 34:7

After the 9/11 attack, my wife began noticing an outbreak of patriotism. One day she mentioned it to me.

"Have you noticed that everywhere you look these days, you see American flags and window stickers with the slogan, 'God Bless America!'?"

"Yes," I replied.

"Well," she continued, "I think that slogan is all wrong!"

"What do you mean?" I asked.

"I mean, God has already blessed this country abundantly. What we now need is not for God to bless us but for us to bless Him. The slogan should read, 'America Bless God!'"

I thought her insight was so profound that I had our ministry's artist design a window sticker with an American flag. Above the flag we put the slogan, "America Bless God!" Beneath the flag we put a reference to 2 Chronicles 7:14, a verse that contains — as we shall see — a formula for national revival.

Patriotism or Repentance?

I suppose the reason my wife's insight impacted me so greatly is because I had been so disappointed by our nation's response to the 9/11 attack. I had hoped it would drive us to our knees in repentance and would serve to turn our hearts back to God. Instead, it seemed to provoke primarily an outbreak of patriotism.

2 Chronicles 7:14

Let's get one thing clear: patriotism is an exercise in pride. God did not allow the 9/11 attack in order to bring about a revival of prideful patriotism. He is calling this nation to repentance, not pride. Our pride is what has gotten us in trouble. He wants to see us humble ourselves before Him and repent of our sins.

Thus far, we seem to have missed that message. Here's how a pastor friend of mine in Northern Ireland expressed the situation to me: "God used 9/11 to set off an alarm clock for America. But I fear that the response has been one of rolling over, hitting the snooze button, and going back to sleep."

"America Bless God!" expresses the proper response — the desperately needed response. And 2 Chronicles 7:14 expresses how we can do that:

> [If] my people who are called by My name humble themselves and pray and seek My face and turn from their wicked ways, then I will hear from heaven, will forgive their sin, and will heal their land.

This is a remarkable passage. God says that there is definitely a way to save a nation from His judgment. The key is repentance. Specifically, we are called to do four things: humble ourselves, pray, seek His face, and turn from our wicked ways. In response He promises to hear, forgive, and heal.

Continuing Relevance

I have often heard people say this passage has no relevance to us today because it was a specific promise which God made to the nation of Israel. It is true that God made some promises to Israel that do not apply to anyone else — like His promise to give them the land of Canaan as an everlasting possession.

But this promise is not an exclusive one for Israel alone — not by a long shot! First, it contains fundamental principles that apply to all peoples and all nations. Second, there are examples in Scripture of the promise applying to nations other than Israel.

The Bible teaches from beginning to end that repentance touches God's heart and that He is always responsive to it. King Hezekiah expressed this truth in a letter he wrote: "The Lord your God is gracious and compassionate, and will not turn His face away from you if you return to Him" (2 Chronicles 30:9). Here's how the Lord Himself summarized these principles in a statement to Jeremiah (Jeremiah 18:5-11):

> 5 Then the word of the Lord came to me saying,
>
> 6 "Can I not, O house of Israel, deal with you as this potter does?" declares the Lord. "Behold, like the clay in the potter's hand, so are you in My hand, O house of Israel.
>
> 7 "At one moment I might speak concerning a nation or concerning a kingdom to uproot, to pull down, or to destroy it;
>
> 8 if that nation against which I have spoken turns from its evil, I will relent concerning the calamity I planned to bring on it.
>
> 9 "Or at another moment I might speak concerning a nation or concerning a kingdom to

build up or to plant it;

10 if it does evil in My sight by not obeying My
    voice, then I will think better of the good with
    which I had promised to bless it.

11 "So now then speak to the men of Judah and
    against the inhabitants of Jerusalem, saying,
    'Thus says the Lord, "Behold, I am fashioning
    calamity against you and devising a plan
    against you. O turn back, each of you from his
    evil way, and reform your ways and your
    deeds."'"

I have reproduced this lengthy passage in full because I
wanted you to read it with your own eyes. It is that important.
It enumerates the same principles contained in 2 Chronicles
7:14, but it spells them out in more detail, and it applies them
to all nations.

The message is clear. The blessings and curses a nation
experiences are determined by that nation's relationship with
God. And even when God responds to an evil nation by
deciding "to uproot, to pull down, or to destroy," He will
change His mind and send blessings if the nation "turns from
its evil."

The Example of Ninevah

A good example of this principle in operation can be found
in the book of Jonah. God commissioned this reluctant prophet
to go to Ninevah, the capital city of the Assyrian Empire, and
preach a message of "Turn or burn!" To Jonah's astonishment, the people listened to his message, and the king led the
entire nation in repenting before the Lord.

The king humbled himself by putting on sackcloth and
sitting on ashes. He then issued a proclamation calling the
whole nation to repentance. In the proclamation he pondered,
"Who can tell? Perhaps even yet God will have pity on us and
hold back His fierce anger from destroying us" (Jonah 3:9 —

NLT). The next verse says that "when God saw their deeds, that they turned from their wicked way, then God relented concerning the calamity which He had declared He would bring upon them" (Jonah 3:10).

The Application to America

This brings us full circle back to the question we started with: Is there any hope for America? The answer by now should be obvious. There is always hope with a God who is "compassionate and gracious, slow to anger, and abounding in lovingkindness and truth" (Exodus 34:6). The apostle Paul refers to Him in Romans 15:13 as "the God of hope."

But He must be approached in faith, humility, and repentance. Any hope America has left depends upon our turning back to God, reaching out to Him in humble faith, and repenting before Him.

There is a powerful song by Squire Parsons that graphically presents the need for our nation to return to God. It is called, "Bring Back the Cross."

> As I watched Old Glory waving
> In the courthouse square,
> She seemed so all alone and fragile,
> Even in despair.
> Her stars had lost her glimmer,
> The stripes her majesty.
> As I thought what is the matter,
> It seemed Old Glory spoke to me.
>
> "Bring back the Cross.
> By myself I cannot stand.
> Bring back the Cross.
> We need the help of God's strong hand."
> Can't you hear Old Glory cry?
> Can't you feel her grief and pain?
> America, bring back the Cross again.

Some might argue that it is too late for America. They may contend that our hearts are too hard. That may be true. But if it is too late, it is not because of God's tender and merciful heart, ready at any time to respond to repentance. If God's judgment falls on America, we will have to bear the responsibility.

What about it? Is it too late for America? For the answer to that question, let's return to our symbolic type in the Scriptures — the nation of Judah.

A Depraved Leader

The darkest period in Judah's history was during the 55 year reign of King Manasseh. The nation was 233 years old when Manasseh came to the throne. The northern nation of Israel had fallen to the Assyrians 25 years earlier. God was sending prophets to warn Judah of the same fate if its people did not repent, but no one was listening. So God gave them the kind of evil leader they deserved as a judgment upon the nation.

In 2 Chronicles 33 we find a listing of the sins of Manasseh. It is a grim list. He wallowed in idolatry, building altars on "high places" throughout the land to honor pagan gods. He dabbled in astrology, in violation of God's Word. He practiced witchcraft and consulted mediums in order to communicate with the dead. He blasphemed God by placing a carved image in God's temple in Jerusalem. And he burned his children alive as offerings to his pagan gods! (2 Chronicles 33:1-7)

"Thus Manasseh misled Judah and the inhabitants of Jerusalem to do more evil than the nations whom the Lord destroyed before the sons of Israel" (2 Chronicles 33:9). This wicked man pulled down the whole nation to his level.

It is reminiscent of the presidency of Bill Clinton who degraded the office with his lies, his sexual misconduct, and his promotion of ungodly causes like abortion and homosexuality. The more he misbehaved, the higher his ratings seemed to go as he dragged the nation down into the gutter with him.

An Amazing Boy

When Manasseh's 8 year old grandson, Josiah, succeeded him to the throne, there appeared to be no hope for Judah. The entire nation, including the priesthood, was caught up in sin.

But a dramatic reversal was about to take place. And it happened all because of something Josiah did when he turned 16. The Word says that in that year — at an age when most young people are rebelling against everything — Josiah "began to seek the God of his father David" (2 Chronicles 34:3).

Incredibly, in the midst of all the evil, Josiah began to evidence his ancestor David's heart for God. As he sought the Lord, he was empowered by God in fulfillment of a promise contained in 2 Chronicles 16:9 — "The eyes of the Lord move to and fro throughout the earth that He may strongly support those whose heart is completely His."

At age 20 Josiah took his first bold step toward turning the hearts of his people back to God. He ordered that the nation be purged of idols. He further ordered that all the altars in the high places be destroyed. Six years later he felt politically strong enough to take on the corrupt priesthood. He ordered that the Temple be cleansed of anything pagan and that it be repaired (2 Chronicles 34:3-7).

A Life Changing Discovery

During the purification of the Temple, something amazing happened. The High Priest discovered the Temple Scroll — the Torah containing the writings of Moses. It had probably been stored behind some pagan statue and then forgotten (2 Chronicles 34:14).

Think about that for a moment. The High Priest had lost the Word of God! Is it any wonder that the nation was in such pitiful shape?

Something equally amazing happened next. The scroll was taken to the king and read to him by one of the scribes. When the king heard the Word of God, he "tore his clothes" in contrition! Isn't that something? The godliest man in the land began to repent when he heard God's Word! What a testimony to the power of the Word (2 Chronicles 34:15-19).

At this point the king became greatly disturbed over the fact that the words he had heard from the writings of Moses indicated that his nation might suffer fatal judgment from the Lord because of the grievous sins of its leaders and its people. He told the priests "to inquire of the Lord as to His intentions" (2 Chronicles 34:20-21).

The priests went to a prophetess named Huldah and told her what the king wanted. She responded by affirming that the king's concerns were justified. She told them that God had made up His mind to pour out His wrath on Judah, but she said He had decided to delay it because of Josiah's reaction to the Word. Here's what she told the priests to tell the king (2 Chronicles 34:27-28):

> 27 Because your heart was tender . . . and
> because you humbled yourself before
> Me, tore your clothes, and wept before
> Me, I truly have heard you [and]

> 28 . . . you shall be gathered to your grave
> in peace, so your eyes shall not see all
> the evil which I will bring on this place
> and its inhabitants.

The king was so blessed by this message and God's Word that he decided to call a national convocation so that the Word of God could be read to all the people. When this was completed, the king stood before the people and formally renewed their covenant with the Lord, promising to obey His commandments (2 Chronicles 34:29-31).

A National Celebration

The only thing left to do was to celebrate. The nation and its leaders had rediscovered their Creator and His Word. They could not contain the joy in their hearts. They proceeded to celebrate the Passover — probably for the first time in anyone's memory.

And what a celebration it turned out to be! Here's how the Bible describes it: "And there had not been celebrated a Passover like it in Israel since the days of Samuel the prophet [over 400 years]; nor had any of the kings of Israel celebrated such a Passover as Josiah did with the priests, the Levites, all Judah and Israel who were present, and the inhabitants of Jerusalem" (2 Chronicles 35:18).

A Story of Hope

I believe this remarkable story provides hope for America. It shows that even when God has made up His mind to destroy a nation for its sin, He is willing to postpone the judgment in response to national repentance. The story also shows that such repentance will lead to national revival.

Let's consider the key elements in Judah's path to repentance and national renewal.

Seeking God

It all began with one person seeking God. This is where spiritual renewal always begins, whether on the part of an individual, a family, a church, or a nation. Someone must have a yearning for God — a desire to draw nearer to Him and to get to know Him better. We must have the attitude of the psalmist who wrote: "As the deer pants for the water brooks, so my soul pants for You, O God. My soul thirsts for God, for the living God" (Psalm 42:1-2).

This attitude will be reflected in an insatiable appetite for God's Word and a commitment to earnest prayer. Every great revival throughout history has come in response to passionate and persistent prayer. The book of James exhorts us to "draw near to God and He will draw near to you" (James 4:8). This admonition is an echo of one in the Old Testament: "[When] you . . . call upon Me and come and pray to Me . . . I will listen to you. You will seek Me and find Me when you search for Me with all your heart" (Jeremiah 29:12-13).

Purging Idols

As we turn toward God, we must turn away from the idols in our lives, just as Josiah purged them from the land of Judah. Our idols may not be as crude and evident as the ones that prevailed in Judah, but they are just as real and just as spiritually debilitating.

Our idols are things like career, family, education, money, sex, nation — the list goes on and on. They are the things that obsess us and ultimately possess us, and thus separate us from God. The apostle Paul urged believers to "flee from idolatry" (1 Corinthians 10:14). Some of the last words the apostle John wrote were these: "Little children, guard yourselves from idols" (1 John 5:21).

Cleansing Temples

The third thing Josiah did was to cleanse the Temple, and that is an essential step in our lives. Since the Cross, believers have served as the temple of God's Spirit, for He indwells us when we put our faith in Jesus (1 Corinthians 3:16).

The Holy Spirit is a wonderful gift, given to empower us, guide us, enlighten us, and encourage us. The problem is that we can grieve the Spirit (Ephesians 4:30) and quench the Spirit (1 Thessalonians 5:19). That means the Spirit can be resident within us without being president over us.

Who is on the throne of your life? You or the Holy Spirit? This is a serious matter, for the apostle Paul wrote: "All who are being led by the Spirit of God, these are the Sons of God" (Romans 8:14).

Reading the Word

Just as Josiah's life was transformed by exposure to the Word of God, so also we must become immersed in the Word. This is the key to spiritual growth, and it is the secret to staying close to God and keeping the Holy Spirit on the throne of our lives. In Psalm 1 we are told that any person who delights in God's Word will be blessed: "He will be like a tree firmly planted by streams of water, which yields its fruit in its season and its leaf does not wither; and in whatever he does, he prospers" (Psalm 1:3).

Our souls were designed to feed upon God's Word. The writer of Hebrews sums up the importance of the Word in this way: "The Word of God is living and active and sharper than any two-edged sword . . . piercing as far as the division of soul and spirit, of both joints and marrow, and able to judge the thoughts and intentions of the heart" (Hebrews 4:12).

Renewal begins by seeking God. It proceeds with the purging of idols. It gains momentum as we cleanse our temples. It deepens as we get into the Word. And it crystallizes as we renew our covenant relationship with God.

Renewing the Covenant

Just as the people of Judah were in a covenant relationship with God, so also are we today who profess to be Christians. We have a New Covenant, one written on our hearts and not on stones. It is a covenant of trust — that we will trust in Jesus as our Lord and Savior.

What is the condition of your covenant relationship? Are you really trusting in Jesus on a daily basis? Or, has your trust been misplaced in money, education, experience, or contacts?

And what about the Lordship of Jesus? Is He really Lord of your life? Is He Lord of your money? Your career? How about your leisure time, your movies, your videos, and your music? Is He Lord of much of anything, or would He have to push you aside in order to assume that position?

Do you need to rededicate your covenant relationship with Jesus, renewing your trust in Him? Isaiah wrote (Isaiah 26:3-4):

> 3 The steadfast of mind You will keep
>   in perfect peace,
>   Because he trusts in You.

> 4 Trust in the Lord forever,
>   For in God the Lord,
>   We have an everlasting Rock.

Experiencing Worship

Renewal experienced must be expressed in praise and worship, just as ancient Judah did. The person who is spiritually renewed *must* worship God, and as he does so, he will be further renewed and strengthened in his spirit.

We were created to worship. One of the surest signs of a spiritually dead person is a lack of enthusiasm for worship. Jesus affirmed this when he told a Samaritan woman, "An hour is coming, and now is, when the true worshipers shall worship the Father in spirit and truth, for such people the Father seeks to be His worshipers" (John 4:23). Think about that! The Father is actively seeking worshipers who will worship Him "in spirit and in truth."

Lessons about God

The experience of Judah under the leadership of Josiah shows that the God of this universe is a personal God who desires an intimate personal relationship with each of us. But He is a gentleman. He will not force Himself upon us. We must reach out and seek Him. When we do so, He will meet us more than halfway, renewing us, strengthening us, and blessing us. Here's how Isaiah expresses it (Isaiah 40:31):

> Those who hope in the Lord
> Will gain new strength;
> They will mount up with wings like eagles,

> They will run and not get tired,
> They will walk and not become weary.

The experience of Judah also makes it clear that God is serious about sin, whether individual or national. He does not overlook rebellion against His Word. He is patient and long-suffering, because He does not wish that any should perish (2 Peter 3:9). But for those who persist in sin, a day of reckoning will come sooner or later. The prophet Nahum expressed this truth in no uncertain terms in a sermon he preached to sinful Ninevah (Nahum 1:2-3):

> 2 A jealous and avenging God is the Lord;
> The Lord is avenging and wrathful.
> The Lord takes vengeance on His adversaries,
> And He reserves wrath for His enemies.
> 3 The Lord is slow to anger and great in power,
> And the Lord will by no means leave the guilty
> unpunished.

Grace or Wrath

John the Baptist declared in one of his sermons that God deals with sin in one of two ways — grace or wrath (John 3:36). Grace is a gift to those who respond to God in faith and repentance. Wrath is reserved for those who turn their backs on God and refuse His grace. This applies to nations as well as individuals.

Again, Judah is a classic example of this truth. Although the nation experienced a great spiritual revival under Josiah, within 10 years after his death, the people of Judah were once again slaves to sin, and their leaders were involved in active rebellion against God. The problem seems to have been that sin had become ingrained in the soul of the nation by the time Manasseh's reign ended. Josiah's revival, therefore, proved to be a temporary one. Because the people persisted in sin, God finally delivered them to destruction at the hands of the Babylonians.

This tragic story should remind us that spiritual renewal must be an ongoing exercise. It is not something that is permanent in nature. That's because we are all leaky vessels. We can be full of the Spirit one day and be sloshing around the next like a half-empty barrel. The practice of holiness is a daily battle requiring daily refreshment in the Word and prayer.

The Example of England

The nation of England is a modern day example of what I am talking about. In the 19th Century, England was the world's center of Christianity. The nation produced great preachers like Charles Spurgeon and great hymn writers like Charles Wesley. The British sent missionaries out all over the world, and they translated the Bible into many languages.

As a nation, the British were blessed with great freedom and prosperity. They were entrusted with the world's greatest empire — one upon which the sun never set.

But early in the 20th Century, English seminaries were invaded by the German School of Higher Criticism espousing its rubbish that the Bible is not God's Word but, rather, is Man's search for God, and is, therefore, full of myth, legend, and superstition. The British bought this lie — hook, line and sinker. The result was the destruction of British Christianity as preachers shoved aside the Word of God and began preaching the wisdom of Man. Today less than 7% of the English people attend church, and many of those are attending churches that are apostate.

As the nation declined spiritually, it also declined politically. The British empire fell apart at the seams, and the nation became a shadow of its old self in power and influence.

The Message for America

America is following the same path trodden by Judah and England. Again, I ask, why should our fate be any different?

Yes, we can still repent and even enjoy a great national revival, as Judah did and as England did in 1904-1905 when the tremendous revival broke out in Wales. But I fear that, like Judah and England, sin has become ingrained in our national soul. I suspect, therefore, that any revival we may experience will prove temporary.

As in the days of Jeremiah, our rebellion against God has become set in stone. Our faces are harder than rock. Our hearts are entrenched in sin, and we have forgotten how to blush.

If written today, the song, "America the Beautiful," would have to be expressed in different words:

America the Beautiful?

O land well known for sex and porn,
For movies filled with filth,
For violence in its schools and streets,
And greed within its heart.

America! America!
God shed His grace on thee,
But you have mocked His majesty
From sea to shining sea.

Coping with Tragedy

In the midst of all the horror of the 9/11 attacks and the devastation of Hurricane Katrina, I have been able to keep an eternal perspective and thus a sense of calm and hope because of something that Psalm 2 reveals.

The psalm says that all the nations of the world are in revolt against the Lord and His Anointed One, the Messiah. It says the national leaders shake their fists at God and say, "Who are You to tell us what we can and cannot do?" It says that the nations are constantly plotting evil, trying to thwart God's will in history. Needless to say, this is not the part of the psalm that comforts me.

What gives me reassurance is the next section of the psalm. It describes God's response to the evil of the nations and their leaders. ***The psalm says God responds by sitting in Heaven and laughing!*** That's right, God sits in Heaven and laughs at the evil plots of Satan and Man. Is it because He does not care? Not at all! It is because He has it all under control.

The psalm says that God has the nations in "derision." That means, once again, that He has the wisdom and power to orchestrate all their evil to the triumph of His Son. The psalm also says that God laughs because He has appointed a day of judgment when He will hold all the evil leaders of the world accountable for their actions.

Our Only Hope

The greatest example of God's ability to bring good out of evil is to be found in the Cross. When Jesus was nailed to the Cross, Satan thought he had gained his greatest success. Psalm 22 pictures Satan and his demonic hordes dancing around the Cross in glee. Since that psalm is prophetic, I'm sure that must have happened, and I'm certain that Jesus must have witnessed it with His spiritual eyes. But within days of the crucifixion, Satan was running for cover because God took the most dastardly act of history and turned it into the most glorious through the power of the resurrection.

What then are we as Christians to do as we face the future? Are we simply to resign ourselves to our nation's ultimate destruction? No! A thousand times, No! We are to pray for our nation and its leaders. We are to stand for righteousness. We are to walk in holiness. We are to share the Gospel. And we are to live clinging to hope, remembering that our hope is not in riches or military power. Our hope, our only hope, is the Lord Jesus Christ.

Chapter 9

Facing A Tough Future:
How can we be overcomers?

"Even though I walk through the valley of the shadow of death, I will fear no evil, for You are with me . . . "— Psalm 23:4

The Bible clearly teaches that society will degenerate in the end times, becoming as evil as it was in the days of Noah (Matthew 24:37-39). The Apostle Paul, speaking as a prophet, says that society will descend into a black pit of immorality, violence, and paganism (2 Timothy 3:1-5). He asserts that men will be "lovers of self, lovers of money, and lovers of pleasure." People will be "boastful, arrogant, and unholy," and children will be "disobedient to parents."

Sounds like the evening news, doesn't it? In short, we have arrived.

Signs of Coming Persecution

We should be deeply concerned over these developments, not only because we are witnessing the destruction of our beloved America, but because both Jesus and Paul prophesied that when these things occur, the Church will come under attack and individual Christians will be persecuted. Jesus said that as lawlessness increases, "most people's love will grow cold" (Matthew 24:12). He stated that in this hostile atmosphere, many professing Christians will "fall away" and will proceed to cooperate in the persecution of their former brothers and sisters in Christ (Matthew 24:10). Paul indicates the same thing when he says that people will be "haters of good" and that they will therefore be "brutal" and "reckless," reviling those who stand for righteousness (2 Timothy 3:2-4).

We are watching these prophecies come true today before our very eyes, both here in America and around the world. As our culture has secularized and paganized, Christianity, the Church, and Christians have come under increasing attack as "intolerant bigots." The attacks are going to intensify, and it is going to become increasingly difficult for Christians to stand for righteousness. Jobs will be lost. Careers will be destroyed. Christians will even be sent to prison for speaking out against evils like homosexuality because such pronouncements will be labeled as "hate crimes."

What then are those of us who love Jesus to do as we face a rising wave of ridicule, harassment, and persecution for our faith? How shall we live for Christ in the end times? Let me suggest a few guidelines.

Order Your Priorities

The starting point is to review your priorities and make certain that God is first in your life. Be honest with yourself. Don't play games. Don't kid yourself.

Most Christians have allowed their priorities to get very mixed up. Usually, job or career is number one, family is second, and God is third or even fourth behind an obsession with sports or something similar.

Ask yourself this question: If God were to give you the opportunity to make one request, what would it be? Would you ask for money? Power? Fame? Success?

Solomon asked for wisdom, but David asked for something ten thousand times more profound — he asked for intimacy with God (Psalm 27:4). And, because he put God first, he states in Psalm 27 that he did not fear life (verse 1) or death (verse 13). It is also the reason that he is remembered as "the man after God's own heart" (Acts 13:22).

Stand on the Word

The Bible says that the end times will be an age of deception (Matthew 24:24, 1 Timothy 4:1, and 2 Timothy 4: 3-4). In fulfillment of that prophecy, we are today being bombarded with false but alluring religious systems offered by the Christian cults, Eastern religions, and the New Age Movement.

Most professing Christians are sitting ducks for spiritual deception because the average Christian is not certain what he believes. And even when he is able to articulate a belief, he usually does not know why he believes it. The result is that a Jehovah's Witness can turn the average Christian into a theological pretzel in two minutes flat.

Anyone can be deceived. If you are to guard yourself against deception, you must get into the Word and stay in it on a daily basis. Also, you must test everything by the Word (1 John 4:1). For Catholics this means discarding doctrines like purgatory that have no basis in the Word whatsoever. For Protestants it means being alert to the twisting of scriptures or the manipulation of verses out of context. On every doctrine, the Bible needs to be searched from Genesis to Revelation to see what is said about the particular topic.

Believe in the Power of God

I am convinced that most professing Christians are deists. A deist is a person who believes in an impersonal god who never intervenes in human affairs. According to Deism, we are supposed to cope with life's problems by using our reason, our talents, and the wisdom of the Scriptures. As far as the deist is concerned, at the end of the First Century, God retired, the supernatural ceased, and the age of miracles came to an end.

But the Hebrew Scriptures teach that God never changes (Malachi 3:6). And the New Testament specifically states that "Jesus Christ is the same yesterday, and today, yes and forever" (Hebrews 13:8).

There is no way we can cope with the evil of end time society in our own strength. Anyone who tries to do so will be defeated. Our only hope is to turn to a God who is alive and well, who is still on the throne, who hears prayer and answers prayer, and who still performs miracles.

We must realize that the Bible teaches that we can limit God by our unbelief. This is a great paradox. Think about it — although God is all-powerful (Luke 1: 37), we who are power-less in comparison can nonetheless limit His power by our unbelief (Mark 6:1-6). That's because God is a gentleman. He does not force Himself upon us. If we want to try to cope on our own, He will let us. He responds when we reach out to Him in faith (James 1:6).

Persist in Prayer

One of the greatest blessings God has given believers is supernatural communication. God cares for us personally (1 Peter 5:7), and He desires to communicate with us (James 4:8). Because He loves us, He earnestly desires our fellowship (John 4:23).

The tragedy is that most professing Christians seem to be inclined to turn to prayer as a last resort — only when all else has failed and the situation has become desperate. Some of this reluctance to seek God in prayer is due to pride, and thus the Scriptures continually exhort us to humble ourselves (1 Peter 5:6). Others fail to depend on prayer because of unbelief. They either think God doesn't care, or else they think He is no longer active in history.

But the Bible says "we do not have because we do not ask" (James 4:2). How many blessings of God have you left on the table because you tried to handle your problems yourself? The Bible also says that "the prayers of a righteous man can accomplish much" (James 5:16). Do you interpret this to mean that the power of your prayers depends on your righteousness? That is not what it means. If you are truly born again, then you are a righteous person because you are clothed in the righteousness of Jesus (Isaiah 61:10).

Rely on the Holy Spirit

Most professing Christians seem to be afraid of the Holy Spirit. This is usually due to a lack of knowledge concerning the Spirit. For example, there is a tendency to write off the Holy Spirit as some sort of impersonal force — like "The Force" in Star Wars.

We need to understand that the Holy Spirit is a person. He is the supernatural presence of God in the world today. He performs a dual role. For the unbeliever, He is God's Evangelist. He is the one who works on human hearts to draw them to the Cross in repentance. No one is saved apart from the testimony of the Spirit (John 6:44 and 65).

With regard to the believer, the Holy Spirit is God's indwelling presence to provide us with power and guidance. He is our Enabler. He is also God's Potter, for one of His basic responsibilities is to daily shape believers more fully into the image of Jesus (2 Corinthians 3:17-18).

One of the ironies of the Christian life is that we cannot serve God in our own power. Rather, the only way we can effectively serve the Lord is by relying on the power of His Holy Spirit who resides within us. The problem is that it is possible to quench and grieve the Spirit (1 Thessalonians 5:19 and Ephesians 4:30).

The Word calls on us to be filled with the Spirit (Ephesians 5:18). This can happen only if we are willing to release the Spirit to become the Lord of our lives. Most of us are content to let the Spirit be resident in our lives. He does not want to be simply a resident; He desires to be president.

Is that the case in your life? Is the Holy Spirit on the throne of your life? Or is He being treated as an unwelcome guest? There is no way you will be able to withstand the pressures of end time society without relying daily on the power of God's

Spirit.

Practice Tough Faith

Faith comes easy when everything is going smoothly. When there is good health and prosperity, it is easy to praise the Lord. The test of faith comes when all the circumstances of life turn sour.

God has not promised believers a rose garden. We live in a fallen world. The rain falls on the just and the unjust. The wicked prosper. Justice seldom prevails.

It is easy for the righteous to grow discouraged. This calls for the practice of tough faith — the kind of faith that is not dependent on circumstances. It's the kind of faith that hangs in there when the going gets tough because of a confident belief that "all things work together for good for those who love the Lord" (Romans 8:28).

God never promises that believers will be immune to suffering. What He does promise is that He will be there to walk through the trials with us. He promises to be beside us when we "pass through the waters" and "walk through the fire" (Isaiah 43:2). And He states that He will be there when we "walk through the valley of the shadow of death" (Psalm 23:4).

What is the quality of your faith? When life turns sour, do you turn to God, or do you question Him or even curse Him? One of the keys to hanging tough is to learn the promises of God's Word (like Philippians 4:6-7, 11-13, and 19) and start claiming them in prayer when confronted with the challenges of life.

Keep an Eternal Perspective

We are to be in the world but not of the world (John 17:11 and 16). That's a difficult principle to follow. It constitutes a daily struggle.

It is so easy to get our eyes off the Lord and focus instead upon the world in which we live. The daily demands are so pressing. And one of the greatest of those demands is that we conform to the world — to the world's language, dress, entertainment, and values.

That's why we are constantly exhorted in Scripture to consider ourselves as "aliens, exiles, and strangers" who are just passing through this world (Hebrews 11:13 and 1 Peter 2:11). We are told to "set our minds on things above, not on the things that are on the earth" (Colossians 3:2). And we are warned to never fall in love with the world or grow comfortable with it (Romans 12:2 and 1 John 2:15-16). In fact, Jesus said we are to "hate our life in this world" (John 12:25), and His brother, James, said "friendship with the world is hostility toward God" (James 4:4).

What does it mean to hate the world? It means we are to hate the evil world system that prevails in society. We are to hate a system that glorifies violence and immorality and which depreciates the value of life.

As C. S. Lewis once put it, "We are to live like commandos behind the enemy lines, preparing the way for the coming of the Commander-in-Chief." In other words, we are to live yearning for the day when Jesus will burst from the heavens to bring peace, righteousness, and justice to the earth.

Look for Jesus

This brings us to the final guideline I would like to emphasize regarding how to live for Jesus in the end times. The Bible tells us point blank that we are to live "looking for Jesus" (Titus 2: 13).

Most Christians are so caught up in the world that they live thinking about anything but the return of Jesus. This is a sad state of affairs because Jesus' return is our "blessed hope" (Titus 2:13). And His return is imminent.

Another problem is that most Christians know so little about Bible prophecy that they cannot get excited about the Lord's return. How can you get excited about an event you know nothing about? Ignorance produces apathy.

And apathy about the Lord's return has tragic consequences. It robs us of an eternal perspective, and it destroys
any sense of urgency about reaching lost souls. It also under-
mines a powerful motivator for holy living.

You see, when a person comes to truly believe that Jesus is
returning and may return any moment, that person will be
motivated to holiness and evangelism. Regarding holiness, the
Apostle John put it this way: "We know that when He appears
[the Rapture], we shall be like Him [glorified] . . . And
everyone who has this hope fixed on Him, purifies himself,
just as He is pure" (1 John 3:2-3). Regarding evangelism,
Peter writes that the only reason Jesus has not yet returned is
because "God does not wish that any should perish, but that all
might come to repentance" (2 Peter 3:9).

A Spiritual Mirror

Paul provides us with a spiritual mirror for end time conduct. He says we are to "deny ungodliness and worldly desires
and to live sensibly, righteously and godly in the present age,
looking for the blessed hope and the appearing of the glory of
our great God and Savior, Christ Jesus" (Titus 2:12-13).

When you look into this mirror, what do you see? Are you
walking in the center of God's will? Have you ordered your
priorities to put God first? Are you standing on the Word of
God, testing everything by it? Do you believe in a personal,
caring and all-powerful God who hears prayers and answers
prayers, and who still performs miracles? Are you relying
daily on the power of the Holy Spirit? Are you practicing
tough faith, refusing to allow the calamities of life to over-
whelm you? Are you keeping an eternal perspective, refusing
to get comfortable with this world? And are you daily looking
for Jesus? Is the Rapture in your heart? Is "Maranatha!" on
your lips?

Postscript

As I bring this book to a close, for what I believe will be the last time, I must admit that I have ambivalent feelings. I am extremely sad, and yet I am full of joyful expectation.

I feel a deep sense of sadness as I see the Great American Experiment in representative government come to an end. We have been abundantly blessed by God over the past 200 years, and we have served as a channel of His blessings to other nations, both as a proclaimer of the Gospel and as a champion of human rights.

Keys to Our Success

One of the secrets to our great success was our commitment to the Judeo-Christian principles revealed in God's Word. Those principles served as the basis of our systems of government, education, and economics.

An even greater reason for our phenomenal success was our commitment to the Gospel of the Lord Jesus Christ. Our forefathers came to this continent in search of freedom to proclaim the Gospel. Our nation was established as a Christian nation. Our relationships were governed by Christian principles. Our laws were based upon God's commandments. The Church, whether Catholic or Protestant, provided us with our reason for being.

Our Track Record

We were far from perfect. We struggled with difficult issues like race relations, women's rights, and the balance between labor and management. But our hearts were in the right place because of the Christian principles which propelled us in the right direction. We steadily made progress in all these difficult areas, and many others.

Throughout the 19th Century we sought to evangelize the American continent, and we sent missionaries to the uttermost parts of the earth.

In the first half of the 20th Century, we soared to great heights as we came to the world's rescue in two world wars. In both cases, we entered these international conflicts for selfless purposes — not to gain territory but to "make the world safe for democracy."

Our Stumbling Point

But at the height of our glory and power, following our victory in World War II, we began to turn our back on God. We took our eyes off the One who had blessed us so abundantly and began to focus on ourselves. We gave our hearts to materialism.

In the process, we began to divorce God from our lives — kicking Him out of our schools and separating Him from our government processes. The secularization of our society became our passion, and the result was increasing paganism in every aspect of life.

Our Persistent Rebellion

We have mocked God. We have given our hearts to idols. We have forgotten the source of our blessings. We have turned a deaf ear to the prophetic voices God has raised up to call us to repentance. We have ignored the remedial judgments He has placed upon us, writing them off to coincidence.

We must now face the consequences of our rebellion. God has stepped back and lowered our hedge of protection. He is allowing evil to multiply. Greed is destroying our economy. Incivility is ripping apart our social structure.

Money has become our god.

Belief in Man has become our religion.

The pursuit of pleasure has become our lifestyle.

And the payoff is nihilism. We are wallowing in despair.

We are destined for destruction. But even as I witness the disintegration of all that I hold dear, my heart is full of joyful expectation because the signs of the times are literally shouting that all of history is about to arrive at its consummation with the return of Jesus.

A Biblical Reminder

My mixed feelings remind me of Jeremiah after his beloved city and temple had been destroyed by the Babylonians and his nation had been taken into captivity. He wrote a funeral lament called Lamentations in which he vented the agony of his heart. But right in the middle of it, in a great act of faith, he suddenly paused and made one of the most hopeful declarations to be found in all of God's Word (Lamentations 3:21-24):

> This I recall to mind,
> Therefore, I have hope.
> The steadfast love of the Lord never ceases;
> His mercies never come to an end;
> They are new every morning.
> Great is Thy faithfulness.
> "The Lord is my portion," says my soul;
> Therefore I will hope in Him. (RSV)

Just like Jeremiah, even as I witness all I love being destroyed around me, I can look to the future with great hope and joyful expectation because of the marvelous promises concerning the future that are contained in God's Prophetic Word.

Some Certainties

Based on those promises, I know with absolute certainty:

That Jesus is returning soon;

That He will defeat all the enemies of God;

That He will establish a worldwide reign that will bring peace, righteousness, and justice to all the nations.

And that all of us who are believers will be given the incredible blessing of ruling with Him.

I can hardly wait. All that is within me yearns for the glorious day very soon when Jesus will break from the heavens.

The New World on the Horizon

The corrupt world system that currently dominates this globe is destined to be destroyed. A new world is coming where there will be no homeless, no poor, and no hungry. Justice will prevail. Fairness and equity will abound.

The nations of that world will be committed to the Lord, and the blessings of the Lord will cover the earth as the waters cover the seas.

It is no wonder that the Apostle Paul wrote: "I consider the sufferings of this present time are not worthy to be compared with the glory that is to be revealed to us" (Romans 8:18).

In the dark days that lie ahead, let us keep in mind that God is on His throne, He still hears prayers, He still answers prayers, and He has the wisdom and power to orchestrate all the evil of Satan and Man to the triumph of Jesus. Keep in mind also that (1 Corinthians 2:9):

No eye has seen,
No ear has heard,
Nor has the mind of Man conceived
What God has prepared for those who love Him.

But God has revealed those things to us in His Word. Cling to those revelations in the days ahead. Cling to His glorious promises, and you will be sustained.

> Oh Lord, our Lord,
> How majestic is your Name in all the earth!
> (Psalm 8:1)

References

Preface

14 "The song, 'America the Beautiful' . . ." Robert Fitzpatrick, "Katharine Lee Bates: Biographical Notes," (www.fuzzylu.com/fal mouth/bates/klbnotes.html).

Introduction

20 "'God Bless America' is the unofficial . . ." Library of Congress, "American Treasures of the Library of Congress," (www.loc.gov/ exhibits/treasures/trm019.html).

Chapter 1: God and the Nations

21 "It was a poem entitled . . ." Mark Twain, "The War Prayer," (www.midwinter.com/lurk/making/war prayer.html).

38 "Abe Lincoln understood . . ." Abraham Lincoln, "Proclamation Appointing a National Fast Day," (http://showcase.netins.net/web/ creative/lincoln/speeches/fast.htm).

44 "On September 24, 1814 . . ." Library of Congress, "American Treasures of the Library of Congress," (www.loc.gov/exhibits/trea sures/trm065.html).

Chapter 2: The Nations in Prophecy

51 "The Lord launched His fulfillment . . ." The Jewish Virtual Library, "Theodor (Binyamin Ze'ev) Herzl," (www.us-israel.org/jsource/bio graphy/Herzl.html).

51 "He went to Paris . . ." The Jewish Virtual Library, "Alfred Dreyfus and 'The Affair,'" (www.us-israel.org/jsource/anti-semitism/Drey fus.html).

51 "This agonizing experience . . ." The Jewish Virtual Library, "The Jewish State by Theodor Herzl," (www.us-israel.org/jsource/Zion ism/herzl2.html).

52 "In the Balfour Declaration . . ." The Jewish Virtual Library, "The Balfour Declaration," (www.us-israel.org/jsource/History/baltoc. html).

52   "By the end of World War II . . ." The Jewish Virtual Library, "Demography of Palestine & Israel, the West Bank & Gaza," (www. us-israel.org/jsource/History/demograhics.html).

54   "Today, there are 5.2 million . . ." The Jewish Virtual Library, "Latest Population Figures for Israel," (www.us-israel.org/jsource/So ciety_&_Culture/newpop.html).

56   "The current land for peace . . ." The Jewish Virtual Library, "Declaration of Principle on Interim Self-Government Arrangements," (www.us-israel.org/jsource/Peace/dop.html).

56   "Yassar Arafat made this crystal clear . . ." Information Regarding Israel's Security (IRIS), "Arafat's Johannesburg Speech," (www. iris.org.il/quotes/joburg.htm).

56   "Arafat had already spelled out . . ." National Unity Coalition for Israel, "The PLO's Phased Plan: Synopsis of the Blueprint for Israel's Destruction," (www.israelunitycoalition.com/archive/April 02/043002_pa_ phased_plan.htm).

57   "There are other indicators." Flavius Josephus, "Jewish Antiquities," Section 1.122 (http://classics.mit.edu/Josephus/j.aj.html).

60   "The result was a series of . . ." Pascal Fontaine, "A New Idea for Europe: The Schuman Declaration: 1950-2000," (http://europa.eu. int/comm/dg10/publications/brochures/docu/50ans/txt03_en.html).

60   "The plan was to pool . . ." Europa, "Treaty Establishing the European Coal and Steel Community," (http://europa.eu.int/abc/ obj/treaties/en/entoc29.htm).

60   "The step toward economic union . . ." Tufts University, "Treaty Establishing the European Community as Amended by Subsequent Treaties," (www.tufts.edu/departments/fletcher/multi/texts/rome/con tents.html).

61   "The culminating step . . ." Europa, "Treaty on European Union," (http://europa.eu.int/en/record/mt/top.html).

61   "Since that time . . ." The home website for the European Union is located at http://europa.eu.int. The EU maintains a U.S. website at www.eurunion.org. An excellent book about the European Union is one by Alan Franklin, a London journalist. It is entitled *EU: Final World Empire* (Oklahoma City, OK: Hearthstone Publishing Co., 2002).

61   "It is hard for most people . . ." Council of the European Union, "Homepage of the Council of the European Union," (http://ue. eu.int/en/main.htm).

61   "The most interesting . . ." Europarl, "The European Parliament On-Line," (www.europarl.eu.int/home/default_en.htm).

62   "The financial branch . . ." European Central Bank, "Homepage of the European Central Bank," (www.ecb.int).

62   "Revenue for the EU . . ." Europa, "Budget Publications [for the EU],"(www.europa.eu.int/comm/budget/infos/publications_en. htm).

62   "One of the main things missing . . ." Eurocorps, "Homepage for the Eurocorps," (www.eurocorps.org/site/index.php?language=en &con tent =home).

63   "Significantly, the European Union . . ." Wikipedia, "Enlargement of the European Union," (http://en.wikipedia.org/wiki/Enlargement _of_the_European_Union)

63   "The main thing this super state . . ." View from the Wall Ministries, "Final Warning: A History of the New World Order," (www.view fromthewall.com/fwch10.htm).

64   "There are many spiritual implications . . ." Author unknown, "How Close It Is." This article provides several photographs of the various spiritual symbols used by the European Union. (http://users.town qr.com/keithw/divine/howcloseitis.htm).

64   "There is a spiritual theme . . ." For an excellent discussion of the spiritual implications of the European Union, see Adrian Hilton's book, *The Principality and Power of Europe* (England: Dorchester House Publications, 1997, second edition in 2000). For ordering information, see: www.adrianhilton.com/nf/mainpagenf.htm.

64   "A former Secretary General . . ." Remarks of Leon Marchal were reported by Dr. William Crampton, executive director of The Flag Institute in York, England. The remarks were made in 1973. The website of The Flag Institute is located at www.flaginstitute.org.

65   "It is no wonder that Vatican . . ." Dr. Ian R. K. Paisley, "'Be the Soul of Europe' — Pope Tells Bishops — 'The Church is the Key to the European Union,'" (www.ianpaisley.org/article.asp?ArtKey= soul).

65   "The EU Anthem . . ." Yggdrasil University, "An Ode to Joy," (www.ddc.net/ygg/etext/ode.htm).

Chapter 3: The Search for America

83   "Like Judah . . ." Center for Disease Control, "Trends in Mortality from Cirrhosis and Alcoholism" (www.cdc.gov/mmwr/preview/mm wrhtml/00000821.htm).

83   "With regard to drugs . . ." National Institute on Drug Abuse, "Info Fact Sheets," (www.nida.nih.gov/Infofax/Infofaxindex.html).

85   "Sixty-five million Americans . . ." Center for Disease Control, "Tracking the Hidden Epidemics, Trends in STDs in the United States 2000," (www.cdc.gov/nchstp/dstd/Stats_Trends/Trends 2000. pdf).

85   "Due primarily to sexual immorality . . ." Wilmington Kids Count, "Children in One Parent Households," (www.dekidscount.org/25 childreninoneparent.html).

90   "When the Civil War broke out . . ." NetHymnal, "Battle Hymn of the Republic," (www.cyberhymnal.org/htm/b/h/bhymnotr.htm).

Chapter 4: The Meaning of 9/11

92   "That's because Islam is . . ." There is an outstanding discussion of the cultural nature of Islam in the book by Robert Morey entitled, *The Islamic Invasion* (Eugene, OR: Harvest House Publishers, 1992).

93   "We are also hated because . . ." For a detailed history of Islamic holy war throughout the history of Islam, see the book by Paul Fregosi, *Jihad in the West* (New York: Prometheus Books, 1998).

93   "As I have often said . . ." David R. Reagan, *Living for Christ in the End Times* (Green Forest, AR: New Leaf Press, 2000).

94   "This fact was summed . . ." Judge Roy Moore, "America the Beautiful?" (www.alliance4lifemin.org/americabeautiful.html).

95   "A graphic illustration . . ." Joe Wright, "A Passionate Prayer for America," (www.lamblion.com/articles/other/gems/Gems-06.php). Note: This prayer was originally written by Bob Russell, pastor of Southeast Christian Church in Louisville, Kentucky. He prepared it for a Governor's breakfast. But it did not gain national attention until Joe Wright read it before the Kansas Legislature.

103   "The first thing that comes to mind . . ." M. W. Hodges, "America's Total Debt Report," (http://mwhodges.home.att.net/nat-debt/debt-nat.htm). Another excellent site for keeping up with the national debt is located at www.brillig.com/debt_clock. It is called "The U.S. National Debt Clock."

103 "At the beginning of the 21st Century . . ." Boudewijn Wegerif, "The U.S. Debt Pyramid Scam," (http://landru.i-link-2.net/monques/debtscam.html).

106 "Only 7% of the British . . ." BBC News, "UK is losing its religion," (http://news.bbc.co.uk/1/hi/uk/1043986.stm).

110 "The author of this great . . ." NetHymnal, "My Country Tis of Thee," (www.cyberhymnal.org/htm/m/c/mctisoft.htm).

Chapter 5: The Message of Katrina

122 "In 2004 a White House . . ." Bill Koenig, *Eye to Eye: Facing the Consequences of Dividing Israel*, (Alexandria, VA: About Him Publishing, 2004).

125 "The economic impact . . ." Bridges for Peace, "Israel's 2005 Disengagement Initiative — Numbers to Know," (www.bridgesforpeace.com/modules/.php?name=News&file=print&sid=2282).

125 "And while this travesty . . ." Anonymous, "Israeli/Palestinian Conflict," (www.libertypost.org).

125 "The withdrawal ended on . . ." National Hurricane Center, "Tropical Weather Summary," (www.nhc.noaa.gov/archive/2005/MIAT WSAT_aug.shtml).

126 "I think it is interesting to note . . ." Southern Decadence, "Southern Decadence 2006: New Orleans," (www.southerndecadence.net).

128 "The Governor of Louisiana . . ." Christian Voice, "Purity Comes to New Orleans," (www.christianvoice.org.uk/Press/press010.html).

128 "In like manner, President Bush . . ." George W. Bush, "Proclamation by the President: National Day of Prayer and Remembrance for the Victims of Hurricane Katrina," (www.whitehouse.gov/news/releases/09/20050908-12.html).

129 "New Orleans City Council President . . ." Christian Voice, "Purity Comes to New Orleans."

129 "No public official in our nation . . ." Abraham Lincoln, "Proclamation Appointing a National Fast Day," (http://showcase.netins.net/web/creative/lincoln/speeches/fast.htm).

132 "This song was . . . " Wikipedia, "Hail Columbia" (http:/en.wikipedia.org/wiki/Hail_Columbia)

Chapter 6: The Ominous Year of 2008

135   "It soared from 5.5 trillion . . ." TreasuryDirect, "Historical Debt Outstanding — Annual 2000 – 2008," (www.treasurydirect.gov/govt/reports/pd/istdebt/histdebt_histo5.htm).

135   "In the process, he became the first President . . ." CBS News, "Text of Bush's Mideast Plan,"(www.cbsnews.com/stories/2002/06/24/national/main513235.shtml).

135   "On October 2, 2001 . . ." Associated Press, "Bush: Palestinian state 'part of vision; if Israel respected," (http://edition.cnn.hu/2001/US/10/02/gen.mideast.us/index.html).

135   "The *New York Times* has since revealed . . ." Jane Perlez and Patrick E. Tyler, "Before Attacks, U.S. Was Ready To Say It Backed Palestinian State," October 2, 2001, (www.nytimes.com).

136   "White House correspondent, Bill Koenig . . ." Stan Goodenough, "The UN Resolution: What price will America pay?"(www.israelmybeloved.com/channel/history_prophecy/article/83), page 2. Most of the material in this article was taken from William R. Koenig's book, *Eye to Eye: Facing the Consequences of Dividing Israel*, (Alexandria, VA: About Him Publishing, 2006).

136   "A month later, on November 10 . . ." "Address by President George W. Bush," (www.state.gov/documents/organization/18967.pdf).

136   "Koenig observes that in that same month . . ." Stan Goodenough, "The UN Resolution: What price will America pay?" page 2.

136   Eight months later . . ." CNN News, "Bush outlines Middle East peace plan," (http://archives.cnn.com/2002/ALLPOLITICS/06/24/bush.mideast.speech/index.html).

136   "The next day the second corporate bombshell . . ." Stan Goodenough, "The UN Resolution: What price will America pay?" page 1.

136   "His detailed policy speech of June 2002 . . ." MidEastWeb, "President Bush's Draft Roadmap to Israeli-Palestinian Peace," (www.mideastweb.org/quartetrm2.htm).

137   "The Lord's final response . . ." Tom Paradis, Associated Press, "Stocks tumble as bailout plan fails in House," September 29, 2008, (http://webserver.desnews.com/article/1,5143,700262692,00.html?pg=2).

138   "The most vulnerable are . . ." "MILNET Brief: E-Bomb - Electro Magnetic Pulse Weapon," (www.milnet.com/e-bomb.htm).

139 "The fact that an electromagnetic pulse . . ." William J. Broad, "Nuclear Pulse I: Awakening to the chaos Factor," *Science*, May 29, 1981.

139 "Scientists began to pay serious attention . . ." Wikipedia, "Electromagnetic Pulse," (http://en.wikipedia.org/wiki/Electromagnetic_ pul se), page 1.

139 "Later calculations showed . . ." Electrical and Computer Engineering Department of The University of New Mexico, "Theoretical Notes: Note 353, March 1985 – EMP on Honolulu from the Starfish Event," (www.ece.unm.edu/summa/notes/TNNotes/TN353.pdf).

139 "The larger scientific community . . ." William J. Broad, "Nuclear Pulse I: Awakening to the Chaos Factor," *Science*, May 29, 1981; "Nuclear Pulse II: Ensuring Delivery of the Doomsday Signal," *Science*, June 5, 1981; "Nuclear Pulse III: Playing a Wild Card," *Science*, June 12, 1981.

139 "In 2001 the United States Congress . . ." "Commission to Assess the Threat to the United States from Electromagnetic Pulse (EMP) Attack," (www.empcommission.org).

139 "In 2008 the Commission released its report . . ." "Report of the Commission to Assess the Threat to the United States from Electromagnetic Pulse (EMP) Attack," April 2008, (www.empcom mission.org/ docs/A2473-EMP_Commission-7MB.pdf).

139 "The chairman of the Commission . . ." Bible Prophecy for Today, "EMP – A Weapon for World War III," September 2008, (http:// bibleprophecyfortoday.wordpress.com/2008/09/28/emp-a- weapon-for-world-war-iii).

140 "Hal Lindsey has summed it up . . ." Hal Lindsey, "EMP attack: Overlooked catastrophe," February 20, 2009, (www.worldnetdaily. com/index.php?fa=PAGE.view&pageId=89476).

140 "As long ago as the early 1960's . . ." Anatoly Zak , "The K Project: Soviet Nuclear Tests in Space," *The Nonproliferation Review*, March 2006.

140 "It has recently been revealed . . ." WorldNetDaily, "Scientist to Congress: U.S. risks 'catastrophe' in nuke EMP attack," July 10, 2008, (www.worldnetdaily.com/index.php?fa=PAGE.view&pageId =69280), page 2.

141 "James J. Shinn, Assistant Secretary of Defense . . ." Ibid.

141 "In an article published in the *Jerusalem Post* . . ." Caroline Glick, "Our World: An urgent memo for the next government," *Jerusalem*

Post, February 16, 2009.

141 "Dr. William Graham, in a report. . ." WorldNetDaily, "Scientist to Congress: U.S. risks 'catastrophe' in nuke EMP attack," July 10, 2008, (www.worldnetdaily.com/index.php?fa=PAGE.view&pageId =69280).

142 "The outstanding public debt . . ." Michael Hodges, "America's Total Debt Report" Michael Hodges, (http://mwhodges.home.att. net/nat-debt/debt-nat-a.htm), page 1. See also: "U.S. National Debt Clock," (http://brillig.com/debt_clock).

142 "Our total debt . . ." Michael Hodges, "America's Total Debt Report," pages 11-12.

142 "In March of 2008 . . ." Ibid., page 9.

142 "Since that time, as housing prices have plummeted . . ." Ibid.

142 "Meanwhile, the average auto loan . . ." Ibid.

142 "The result is that 76% of undergraduates . . ." Ben Woolsey and Matt Schulz, "Credit Card Industry Facts, Debt Statistics, 2006-2009," (www.creditcards.com/credit-card-news/credit-card-industry -facts-personal-debt-statistics-1276.php), page 2.

143 "Overall, over 150 million Americans . . ." Money-Zine.com, "Credit Card Debt Statistics" (www.money-zine.com/Financial-Plan ning/Debt-Consolidation/Credit-Card-Debt-Statistics), page 2.

143 "What is particularly disturbing . . ." Michael Hodges, "America's Total Debt Report," page 9.

143 "The result is that the average American household in 2008 . . ." Money-Zine.com, "Credit Card Debt Statistics," page 2.

143 "One expert on American debt . . ." Michael Hodges, "America's Total Debt Report," page 13.

143 "Even more alarming . . . WorldNetDaily, "How big is $1 trillion, really?" (www.worldnetdaily.com/index.php?fa=PAGE.view&page ld=87563).

143 "It is almost impossible . . ." Ibid.

144 "He claims his American mother . . ." Steven Waldman, "Obama's Fascinating Interview with Cathleen Falsani"(http://blog.beliefnet. com/stevenwaldman/2008/11/obamas-interview-with-cathleen. html), page 2.

144 "In his autobiography . . ." The American Humanist Association, "President Obama: Living Proof that Family Values Without Reli-

gion Build Character," (www.americanhumanist.org/Obama-Ad_low.pdf).

144　"In March of 2004 . . ." Steven Waldman, "Obama's Fascinating Interview with Cathleen Falsani."

144　"In it he revealed . . ." Ibid., page 3.

144　"In 1987 he joined the church . . ." Ibid.

144　"As the syndicated columnist . . ." Cal Thomas, "Barack Obama is Not a Christian," June 2, 2008, (http://foxforum.blogs.foxnews.com/2008/06/02/barack-obama-is-not-a-christian), page 2.

145　"Obama made it very clear . . ." Steven Waldman, "Obama's Fascinating　Interview with Cathleen Falsani," page 2.

145　"When Falsani asked Obama . . ." Ibid., page 5.

145　"When asked if he prayed often ..." Ibid., page 4.

145　"Obama also admitted . . ." Ibid., page 8.

145　"Falsani was so shocked . . ." Ibid.

146　"She then asked Obama . . ." Ibid., page 9.

146　"Falsani concluded her remarkable interview . . ." Ibid., page 10.

146　"Joseph Farah, the editor . . ." Joseph Farah, "Barack Obama: Never a Christian," (www.wnd.com/index.php?fa=PAGE.printable&pageId =78757), page 3.

147　"With regard to sexual perversion . . ." The White House, "Support for the LGBT Community," (www.whitehouse.gov/agenda/civil_rights). Note: LGBT is an acronym for Lesbian, Gay, Bisexual and Transgendered.

148　"With regard to abortion . . ." The White House, "Reproductive Choice," (www.whitehouse.gov/agenda/women).

148　"In fact, he promised Planned Parenthood . . ." Americans United for Life, "Fight FOCA," (www.fightfoca.com).

148　"According to pro-choice advocates . . ." Ibid.

Chapter 7: International Stage-Setting

151　"As planned, the European Union . . ." Wikipedia, "Enlargement of the European Union," (http://en.wikipedia.org/wiki/Enlargement_of_the_European_Union), page 2.

151   "These changes were agreed to in . . ." Wikipedia, "Treaty of Nice," (http://en.wikipedia.org/wiki/Nice_Treaty).

151   "On January 1, 2007 . . ." Wikipedia, "Enlargement of the European Union," page 3.

152   "The EU is based upon . . ." Wikipedia, "History of the European Union," (http://en.wikipedia.org/wiki/History_of_the_European_Union), pages 1-5.

152   "To clarify these treaties . . ." Wikipedia, "Treaty Establishing a Constitution of Europe," (http://en.wikipedia.org/wiki/European_Constitution).

152   "The Constitution was intended . . ." The Human and Constitutional Rights Resource Page, "EU Constitution: the State of Play," (www.hrcr.org/hottopics/EuropeanC.html).

152   "But to the astonishment . . ." Wikipedia, "History of the European Union," page 6.

152   "In March of 2007 . . ." Wikipedia, "Berlin Declaration (2007)," (http://en.wikipedia.org/wiki/Berlin_Declaration_(2007).

153   "In December of 2007 . . ." Wikipedia, "Treaty of Lisbon," (http://en.wikipedia.org/wiki/Treaty_of_Lisbon).

153   "Perhaps the most important change . . ." Ibid., pages 14-15.

153   "The Irish decided . . ." Ibid., page 1.

153   "Thus far, the EU leaders . . ." BBC News, "Q&A: The Lisbon Treaty," (http://newsvote.bbc.co.uk/mpapps/pagetools/print/news.bbc.co.uk/2/hi/europe/6901353.stm?ad=1).

154   "The nation of Turkey . . ." Wikipedia, "Accession of Turkey to the European Union," (http://en.wikipedia.org/wiki/Accession_of_Turkey_to_the_European_Union).

155   "His name is Recep Tayyip Erdogan . . ." Wikipedia, "Recep Tayyip Erdogan,"(http://en.wikipedia.org/wiki/Recep_Tayyip_Erdo%C4%9Fan).

155   "In 1997 he was imprisoned . . ." Ibid., page 3.

155   "Since becoming Prime Minister . . ." Ibid., page 2.

156   "After the 1991 collapse . . ." David J. Lynch, *USA Today*, "Russian brings revitalized economy to the table," (http://www.usatoday.com/money/world/2006-07-12-russia-cover-usat_x.htm), page 1.

156   "By 1998 . . ." Ibid., page 2.

156 "The crisis forced . . ." Ibid.

156 "But the true resurgence . . ." Wikipedia, "Vladimir Putin," (http://en.wikipedia.org/wiki/VladimirPutin), page 1.

156 "Oil export revenue . . ." "Russia brings revitalized economy to the table," page 2.

156 "Putin wisely decided . . ." The Energy Information Administration of the U.S. Government, "Russia," (http://www.eia.doe.gov/cabs/Russia/Background.html), page 1.

157 "Between 2000 and 2007 . . ." Ibid.

157 "Even so, at the beginning of 2009 . . ." Yelena Fabrichnaya, *Guardian News,* "Ulyukayev sees rouble around 39-41/basket in near term," February 16, 2009, (www.guardian.co.uk/business/feed article/8360984), page 1.

157 "That's because Putin spent . . ." Peter Baker, *Washington Post,* "Putin Moves to Centralize Authority," September 14, 2004, (www.washingtonpost.com/wp-dyn/articles/A17838-2004Sep13.html), page 1.

157 "He engineered a new electoral law . . ." Luke Harding, *The Guardian,* "Supreme court ban on liberal party wipes out opposition to Putin," March 24, 2007, (www.guardian.co.uk/world/2007/mar/24/russia.lukeharding), pages 1-2.

157 "And he acquired legislation . . ." Wikipedia, "Vladimir Putin," page 15.

157 "The first thing Medvedev did . . ." Wikipedia, "Dmitry Medvedev," (http://en.wikipedia.org/wiki/Dmitry_Medvedev, page 5.

158 "Putin refers to the new . . ." Peter Baker, "Putin Moves to Centralize Authority," page 2.

158 "Others have characterized it as . . ." Ibid. See also: Stephen Kotkin, Foreign Policy Research Institute, "Russia Under Putin: Toward Democracy or Dictatorship?" March 2007,(http://www.fpri.org/enotes/200703.kotkin.russiademocracydictatorship.html).

158 "The best description . . ." Bret Stephens, *Wall Street Journal,* "For the Sake of One Man," July 17, 2007, (http://online.wsj.com/article/SB118463398015768385.html?mod=googlenews_wsj).

158 "While there, he signed an agreement . . ." BBC News, "Russia-Iran nuclear deal signed," February 27, 2005, (http://news.bbc.co.uk/2/hi/middle_east/4301889.stm), page 1.

158   "He took advantage of the occasion . . ." The Associated Press, "In Iran, Putin Warns U.S." October 16, 2007, (http://www.msnbc.msn. com/id/21316255), page 1.

158   "Later that year, in December . . ." Joseph Farah, *WorldNetDaily*, "Russia Equips Iran for War," December 2, 2005, (www.worldnet daily.com/news/article.asp?ARTICLE_ID=47696), page 1.

159   "When the Russians invaded Georgia . . ." Nathan Gardels. *The Huffington Post*, "Brzezinski: Russia's Invasion of Georgia is Reminiscent of Stalin's Attack on Finland," August 10, 2008, page 1, (www.huffingtonpost.com/nathan-gardels/brzezinski-russias-inva si_b_118029.html).

159   "Brzezinski went on to conclude . . ." Ibid.

161   "A new voice on the Bible prophecy scene . . ." Bill Salus, *Isralestine: The Ancient Blueprints of the Future Middle East* (Crane, MO: Anomalos Publishing, 2008)

163   "On January 8, 2009 . . ." *OilVoice*, "Noble Energy Announces Significant Natural Gas Discovery Offshore Israel," (http://www.oil voice.com/n/Noble_Energy_Announces_Significant_Natural_Gas _Dis covery_Offshore_Israel/a7ad3a4a.aspx).

163   "A month later . . ." *Oil in Israel*, "Haifa Gas Discovery Bumped to 5 Trillion Cubic Feet," February 10, 2009, (http://www.oilinisrael. net/ oil-in-israel-articles/haifa-gas-discovery-bumped-to-5-trillion-cubic-feet).

Chapter 8: The Only Hope for America

172   "In the proclamation . . ." *Holy Bible: New Living Translation* (Wheaton, IL: Tyndale House Publishers, 1996).

173   "There is a powerful song . . ." Squire Parsons, "Bring Back the Cross," (http://www.squire parsons.com/).

Additional
Bible Prophecy
Study Resources

Dr. Reagan's Comprehensive Book About Bible Prophecy

What is the destiny of planet earth?

What is going to be the fate of mankind?

We don't have to guess. The Bible spells out God's plan for the ages in great detail through prophecies given thousands of years ago.

In this book Dr. Reagan presents a panoramic survey of the fundamentals of Bible prophecy, with a focus on the prophecies that relate to the end times. In the process, he reveals God's plan for the redemption of mankind and the restoration of the creation.

The book is written in a down-to-earth, easy-to-understand style. Although all the chapters relate to the overall theme, each chapter is designed to stand alone. This makes it possible for you either to read the book straight through or to skip around, reading only those chapters whose topics appeal to you.

The book is divided into five parts: Prophetic Significance, Prophetic Issues, Prophetic Viewpoints, Prophetic Signs, and Prophetic Hope. There is a Prophetic Epilogue in which Dr. Reagan presents an in-depth, verse by verse explanation of Psalm 2, one of the Bible's greatest passages about the Second Coming of the Lord.

The book contains 42 chapters and runs 415 pages in length. It sells for $15. You can order a copy by calling 1-800-705-8316, Monday through Friday, 8am to 5pm Central time. You can also purchase the book through the Lamb & Lion website at www.lamblion.com.

Dr. Reagan's Children's Book About Bible Prophecy

This book is designed for pre-school and elementary children. It focuses on the blessings God has promised the world when Jesus returns.

The book is beautifully illustrated in full color by a gifted Christian artist. It has a large format (8½ x 11"). It is 28 pages in length and has a durable cover. The book contains teaching tips for parents, together with a list of Scripture references. There is one outline page for coloring.

This book would make a wonderful gift for your children or grandchildren. It would also serve as a good presentation item for children in recognition of outstanding achievement in Sunday School or Scripture memorization. $10. ($7 each in quantities of 10 or more.)

Dr. Reagan's Commentary on the Book of Revelation

This book provides a chapter-by-chapter, down-to-earth explanation of the book of Revelation.

It is an easy to understand book that was written for the layman. It is designed to clear away the mystery of Revelation, showing what it means about the future while making it relevant to daily living in the present. It contains many helpful charts and diagrams. 240 pages, $15.

Dr. Reagan's Outline of Messianic Prophecy

The second edition of Dr. Reagan's detailed analytical outline of all Messianic prophecy concerning both the First and Second Advents of Jesus. Every Messianic prophecy in the Bible, both Old Testament and New Testament, is identified and categorized.

The book is printed in a large format (8½ x 11"), and it has a special type of binding that allows the book to lie flat when it is opened. The book runs 135 pages in length. $15.

Dr. Reagan's Book about End Time Living

One of Dr. Reagan's most thought provoking books. It begins with a hard-hitting presentation of the special challenges that Christians face at the beginning of the 21st Century due to the decay of society and increasing apostasy in the Church.

The book then presents ten principles that Christians can follow to overcome paganism and live victorious lives.

The final two chapters present prophetic material from the Bible which shows that we will ultimately triumph over paganism when Jesus returns in glory and power to reign over all the world from Mount Zion in Jerusalem. 264 page. $15.

Video Programs

Lamb & Lion Ministries produces a great variety of video programs in a variety of formats, including interviews, teaching, and preaching.

You can find these listed on the ministry's website at www.lamblion.com. Or, you can call the ministry at 1-800-705-8316, Monday through Friday, 8am to 5pm Central time and request a free copy of the ministry's magazine of Bible prophecy resources.

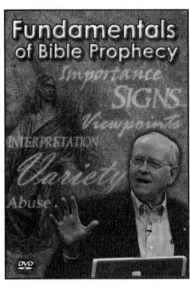

Dr. Reagan's Video about the Fundamentals of Bible Prophecy

This video album contains six presentations made before live audiences by Dr. Reagan. They provide a comprehensive introduction to all the fundamentals of Bible prophecy:

The Abuse of Prophecy
The Importance of Prophecy
The Interpretation of Prophecy
The End Time Viewpoints
The Signs of the Times

The teaching sessions are great for individual study, but they can also be used for study by Sunday School classes and home Bible fellowship groups.

Each video segment runs 25 minutes in length. The album contains two DVDs. One of the DVDs contains printable files for a teacher's manual and student study guides. $25.